Rendezvous with Life

Rendezvous with Life

A Journey through Time

Nirmal Rathore Bikaner

PARTRIDGE

A Penguin Random House Company

To order additional copies of this book, contact
Partridge India
000 800 10062 62
www.partridgepublishing.com/india
orders.india@partridgepublishing.com

FOREWORD

It gives me immense pleasure in writing a foreword for "Rendezvous with Life", authored by Ms Nirmal Rathore. In our day to day life, one comes across numerous situations, yet our reaction to each event is different. The author has expressed her creative prowess by going beyond the routine and has inscribed meanings to each and every moment, which she saw and felt as a poet's inner soul, and expressed in words which has given the right meaning and a subtle message to every reader of this book.

I am proud to see the author, who is married to an army officer, making creative use of the time at her disposal. I have gone through her profile and am genuinely amazed to see her versatility and hidden talents. She is an Artist with a flair for oil and water colour, besides being a national level shooter.

Her work in question gives an insight into various contemporary issues bothering our society and the country. She has touched upon generally each and every aspect of the society. From the "Veil (The Purdha)" to " Yes we Can", she expresses her desire and life force in day to day life. Her satire "Marionette or master of mobiles" on the new age development of mobile and internet technology, to the burden on our children to perform "The 100 Percentile" aptly expresses the malady of our times. The patriotic fervor of the Army and NSG (National Security Guard) touched me. The book is an inspiration for one and all from house wife to a political leader, from a soldier to a child. The message is to work hard, be honest, aspire to be great and have respect for the women, country and self.

SUBHASH JOSHI, IPS
DG, BSF

FOREWORD

Greetings from the House of Mewar!!!

I am delighted to know that your book of poems titled **"Rendezvous with Life"** is dedicated towards the society environment and some extent to the life in Army expressing different experiences, situations dealt with sense and sensibility.

I firmly believe that this initiative in the form of book is not only extremely admirable but also a huge first step in the right direction. The commitment and work being undertaken by you is of immense value to all of us across the country. The idea to have such publication pre-suggests perseverance towards the cause, commitment towards the community that is truly commendable.

The narrative words in the poems 'Woman of Substance!", 'Yes We Can!', 'Music for Soul' 'Black Cat Commandos', Pursuit for a Visionary and Missionary', Mom the Dear—Epitome of Love' are soulful and expressive.

I would like to thank you for inviting me to write something about the book which is indeed a tryst with self, society and destiny. I wish you all round success for your future endeavors.

With Best Wishes.

Lakshyaraj Singh Mewar
Executive Director—HRH
Eternal Mewar
The Palace

FOREWORD

"Rendezvous With Life"

Nirmal Jija never ceases to amaze me ('Jija' is respectful word for an elder sister in Rajasthan).

A housewife handling the turbulences of an army life, parenting two adolescent boys, painting professionally and successfully, a daughter in law, a sister, writing articles and in the midst of all, putting together a collection of poems, which are a reflection of her thoughts on the subjects that have touched heart or crossed her mind.

She writes on subjects common and diverse, earthy and urbane, many that we should have glanced through without batting an eyelid. But to hold your mind on them, to dwell and bring out various aspects of those subjects in the form of poems requires a creative mind, only a body that's selfless, self-assured can devote such time and energy. I respect and admire this ability. This is what makes people like her, beyond ordinary.

Her poems are fun too; I found a phrase in "100 percentile" so aptly describing my state in student life. While you enjoy reading her poems, think of the possibilities you can achieve, Impossible is only in your mind, to quote from one of her poems:

"Mission possible—only possible with trust and faith.
Only when you learn to obey—you can lead.
Only when you learn to listen—you can speak.
And only when you learn to trust—you can win and succeed"

Col Rajyavardhan Singh Rathore, AVSM
Awarded Padam Shri by President
Khel Ratna, Arjuna Award

FOREWORD

'The sentiments expressed by Nirmal Rathore are beautifully summarized by the apt title of the book, "Rendezvous with Life"—it is an honest reflection of the everyday occurrences in live but to capture and express it through words of poetry allows us to connect and find some glimpses of personal reference in her work. It is also a dissemination of ideas, thoughts and emotions, allowing us a sneak peek into the lives of women and their valued sentiments."

Wishing you both well.

Warm Regards,

Raghavendra Rathore
International Designer

POETS NOTE

"Rendezvous with Life" is an ensemble of poems, a flight of fantasy, expressing different experiences, situations dealt with sense and sensibility. Hailing from the 'Royal blood of Bikaner', an artist by profession and passion a dreamer by nature, an iconoclast by conduct, the verses and couplets reflects the moods and moments, splashes of varied colours, replete with creativity and dexterity. This book is indeed a tryst with self, society and destiny.

The genesis of this poetry book is a heartfelt gratitude, towards my life partner for gifting me diamonds, which touched my heart and soul, tickling the rhyme and rhythm of writing prowess which was lying latent for years. As an English Lecturer, I've read and taught enough, but this deep seated wish, dream came true and through by this gift and resulted in my first poem "Necklace—The Marvelous". Some poems are romantic, some inspiring, a few are satire on system, values and human tendencies. 'Yes we can' was inspired by President Obama's famous phrase. 'Being Human' is a take on a cause espoused by Salman Khan, after an interaction with him at NSG (National Security Guard). 'Hope Against Hope' has optimistic fervor, "Veil—The Purdha—is a sound protest, 'Million Dollar Smile" is a satire on man dominated society, "Heroic Rajput Heroines" is a song of glory and valour of a bygone era.

> "The woods are lovely dark and deep
> But I have promises to keep
> And miles to go before I sleep
> And miles to go before I sleep—"

> (Robert Frost)

I wish this symphony, this fountain of ideas keep flowing, satisfy and entertain my readers, the kindling minds who feel for self, society, nation, global world, as one entity (Vasudeo Kutumbakum)

God bless us all

Nirmal Rathore

Contents

"BEING HUMAN"

'Being human'—is the crux of mankind
God's ultimate creation, one of its kind,
Possessing Godly qualities, after the grind
Purest heart and soul, passion, compassion and mind.

'Being human'—is the essence of Mankind
Truth, virtue, fraternity, we should strive and find,
Invoke en-masse to have faith and quest—truth should triumph
Start the pursuit and voyage, finally—truth will triumph.

'Being human'—is the appeal to mankind,
Leave aside country, caste, creed—let's bind,
Forget hierarchy, boundaries, blunders—all faux pas
Be like phoenix—reliving from its own ash.

'Being human'—is the slogan for mankind
Rise above being Bacchus and Maenad—God's of wine,
Eradicate the malice, grotesque, cruelty of the world
Transform, humanity by humility, the genesis of the world.

'Being human'—is the quest of the mankind
Nurture with love, hope, trust—all will be fine,
Rise above Zenith—the ultimate horizon
Man—You are the warrior, savior, Gods son.

'Being human'—is the conquest of mankind
Man—You are the king, emperor—the conqueror,
Be the connoisseur of life, not just food
Don't be just couturiers, but be designer of life—you dude.

Nirmal Rathore Bikaner

'Being human'—is the zeal and zest of mankind
Déjà vu—the feelings, emotions, experiences of life,
Think more than sartorial or tonsorial-oh cupid!
Live for a cause—high aims and ambitions—oh stupid!

'Being human' is the crux of mankind
God's ultimate creation—one of its kind.

HOPE AGAINST HOPE!!

When the catastrophe happens—Hope against hope!
Even when the heavens fall—Hope against hope!
When the dreadful night, engulfs completely,
The Sun will rise, next morn—bright, lustrous, shining.

When the mind is thoroughly paralyzed with fear
And the heart and soul, sinking with despair,
Man! Don't give up! Hope against hope!
Hold your horses, take control of reins or ropes.

When grief is unbearable, believe in belief
Calm your senses, de-stress, try for relief,
God alone knows, the ups and downs of our destiny
Curb your anxiety and sensitivity, escape minds mutiny.

Be thy master, O man! Realize your power
You are the son of God, recall the call of the hour,
Life's ocean has varied—up and down tides
Hug yourself, love yourself and hold thy tight.

Today's fortune will differ from tomorrows
Tomorrow will be definitely better—no sorrows,
Future is always better, than past and present
But life's so precious, let's not waste our present.

The tears are valueless, timeless—so precious
Let's gulp it, as a pinch of salt—no pressures,
The passions, emotions to be understood logically
Let's not be emotional fools, always reacting emotionally.

Strong mind and character ought to be practiced
Brave and bold hearts, peaceful soul, no malice,
In the testing times, give God a chance
To pat your shoulder, with a smiling glance.

Nirmal Rathore Bikaner

Lord oh lord! Thou art a difficult task master
You've tried my patience, courage and power,
I was dreaming on seventh heaven, now on Mother Earth
Boasted of bravery, tough torso—now I know my worth.

Every single day is a battle of honour and survival
Experiences of situations, self realization—destiny's arrival,
Happiness and sorrow—life's fait accompli
Success and failure—truly life's fait accompli.

When the catastrophe happens—hope against hope!
When the heaven's fall—Hope against hope!

FAREWELL TO ARMS

Farewell to Arms, is the need of the hour!
East or West, Northern or Southern
All humans are Gods son, logically brothers,
Different continents or different countries
Have different caste, creed, colour or communities.

Farewell to arms; is the need of the hour!
The frontiers, boundaries, check posts created by man
The faith, belief, honesty, integrity; deceived by men,
Though same blood, flesh; face features differ
Can't we live with peace & harmony? Oh duffer.

Farewell to arms; is the need of the hour!
Hundreds & thousands employed in defence
Waiting to pounce on each other's trivial offence,
The infinite bullets, gun powder, rocket launchers loaded
Pointing eyeball to eyeball, dying for blood shed.

Farewell to arms; is the need of the hour!
Sons become soldiers, some became martyr
Body, heart & soul, dies, cries the kith & kin of martyr,
Whom are we fighting with? And for what reason?
Let's take a pledge, make our motto & mission.

Farewell to arms; is the need of the hour
The last breath stops, but not the war monger
The last soldier is sacrificed, still war looming,
Have the mothers given birth to brave sons for death?
Rather than farewell to Arms & Ammunition—She bids farewell to
    her own son's arms.

Nirmal Rathore Bikaner

Farewell to arms; is the need of the hour
The throbbing of heart beats and the gush of blood
The scars and wounds, tell the story of young blood,
The brave moments, memories of loved ones becomes history,
Let's shun the bloodshed and war, create a new history

Farewell to arms; is the need of the hour!
Our vision, motto and mission

I DARE

I dare; to speak the truth
Even if it pleases or displease, I've taken an oath,
No matter how bitter or better it turns
Even if it exposes one or annoys some with heart burns.

I dare; not to be a sycophant
Telling meaningless tales with no sensible context,
Rule No 1-Boss is always right
Actually, boss is not always right and fully justified.

I dare; to be honest
Kill all evils of mortals, learn to be just,
Wage a war against stealth and corruption
Lead the masses, no mercy for dishonesty, take action.

I dare; not to be callous and complacent
Fight for fellow being, be kind and benevolent,
Let's not accept anything & everything on the platter
Think, evaluate, analyze and rationalize the matter.

I dare; to be daring and courageous
Come what may, from luck or destiny, be gorgeous,
Inspire, ignite, the underdogs and coward
They should feel for humanity, camaraderie-Come lets forget.

I dare; not to be egocentric or selfish
Forget false egos, live selfless life; is my wish,
Many out of the masses are eating, drinking, are merry
Doomed are, some of our country men, I feel so sorry.

I dare; to be affluent & powerful
Work till the last light, for poor & merciful,
Balance the social system, no discrimination
Enhance the value of everyone's life, this is my determination.

I dare; not to follow the wrong path
Create new roads of progress, even if it's a lonely path,
Hurdles & obstacles cannot stop my spirits
Rather following clowns lead a path that befits

I dare; to beckon & summon
The hooligans, destroying the nations harmony,
Let this Universe be united
The world, cosmos, be peaceful & delighted.

I dare; not to be scared of destiny
God's blessing is unlimited, stop this mutiny,
Live life to the fullest
God gives, all of us-The best possible best!

VEIL—THE PURDAH— SHACKLES OF WOMANHOOD

(Inspired by Experience-back home in Rajasthan)

Gods most exemplary creation is Eve-The women
Before its creativity life was lifeless for—Adam,
Beauty, love, luck, grace, humility, humanity
All possible adjectives fall short for this beauty.

The beautiful face with wonderful heart
The royal looks along with utmost loyalty,
The regal persona and personality-par excellence
But why at all cover the face, by veil—a real nuisance!

All humans are born equal with body, heart and soul
Man may be great warrior, with brave role,
Alexander or Hercules, Bheesma or Arjun
Can any one deny Joan of Arc, Jhansi ki Rani and many more.

There's a big fight within me—why this veil?
Why this discrimination with women—are they so frail,
Are we still in slave dynasty, still traditions slave?
Gone are the days of purdah—its absurd and obsolete.

The fair sex—the better half is better equipped
Men need not fool them, in the name of protection,
By keeping veil of thin fabric, is it bullet proof?
Few men with vicious and heinous mentality needs to improve.

Some men have the notorious mind; needs to be controlled
So curb him and put him in shackles and bind him,
Free poor damsels from bonded slavery of purdah
To hide herself and face, as if she's a criminal.

This unfair, unreasonable traditions have done great damage
The better half, life partner, seldom thinks and manage,
'Coz she's dominated for so long, yet to realize
She too has equal right, brains and desires to materialize.

The dormant wishes, dreams, desires, die everyday
On the mercy of her master—The man, what a tragedy!
Born to a women—Man-wants to rule his own creator
Forgets his very being; birth-is because of a women-his mother.

Now let's loose the age old useless ritual
Live with liberty, freedom from hopeless tradition,
Modern world shows such obscene revelations
Let girls give up veil, show their grit, gusto and their brave face.

YES WE CAN

Yes we can! Choose to create a Hell or Heaven
Create history by miracles, or horror by guns,
United we stand—fight terrorism
Ignite the feelings of patriotism—forget 9/11, 26/11.

Yes we can! Finish the cancer of corruption
Judge ourselves and truly do the evaluation,
Mark our deeds and monitor mental pollution
And foremost, realize the magnitude of population.

Yes we can! Wage a war or avoid world war
Punish, or hang the culprit or put behind bar,
The laws ought to be strict; stern judiciary
No bribes, prejudices, bias or beneficiaries.

Yes we can! Protect girl child and women
The mother, sister or daughter of man,
Give them love, pride, freedom—Life's essence
She becomes a daring darling—Women of substance.

Yes we can! Live and let live, our next generations
Blooming buds of happy families, avoid separations,
Being human, adorable, perfect citizens
Nurture and kindle brotherhood, avoid partitions.

Yes we can! Educate one and all poor or rich
No reservations, but on merit becomes Richie Rich,
True genius left in the rut, some get 100 percent
The adolescent is perplexed—forgets past, future and present.

Yes we can! Make a Vivekanand or a Rabindranath Tagore
A friend, philosopher, guide—Great fellows,
Imitate Lord Rama, Lord Krishna—the saviors
Be truthful, with dignified conduct and behaviors.

Yes we can! Hold the horses of Sun God
Be bold like Bheesma, Karan, Arjun or the Lords,
Duty unto death, despite loads of Ashtra
Daring ultimate weapons—Sudarshan Chakra or Bharmastra

Yes we can! Dare to be truthful, today
Be courageous to the core till—Doom's day,
Live life king size, but with gratitude
Kill all Anger, Angst and Attitude
Yes We Can!

OBSESSIONS & CONFESSIONS

Liking & loving someone, more than self
Adoring endlessly is infatuation, love selfless,
Beyond a point, when love hurts; is obsession
Passions, emotions beyond control, lead to confession!

Obsession—for a life partner-a soul mate
Loves, lives for the sake of love, even at closed gates,
Relations, family ties so tough; yet fragile
Extremes occur—lover morose, excited or agile.

Confession is the remedy and the only cure
After all wrong doings, human confesses to God—so pure,
The heavy heart and the troubled soul is relieved
Man realizes his blunders, tries to re-live.

Obsession—for power or absolute power
Leads to frustration and depressive hour,
Absolute powers corrupts absolutely
No feelings, no love lost, man blind folded—truly.

Confession—is the simplest tool for guilt and forgiveness
Solitude-the only way of regret & regress,
Listen to your soul and the inner voice
Give God a chance & let conscience guide you; as last choice.

Obsession—for cash, car or any commodity
Is trivial thinking, as base as infidelity,
Yearning for beauty, love and money
Learn to live gracefully, don't be gawky; honey!

FLOWER SELLER'S PLIGHT

God is omnipresent, and omnipotent!
But how could he miss, poor flower seller's plight,
A tender age, with a longing wish to sell all roses-what a sight!
Alluring & advising passerby, to gift his flowers to their beloved;
    reality bites.

What a juxtaposition!
A comedy of tragedy, what plight,
A little boy running & twisting between cars on Red light
Elsewhere, would have been playing with cars, guns or kites.

God! Don't be so heartless & ruthless
Throwing orphans on roads-so unsafe & insecure
Earning livelihood in poverty, future so obscure
His meager income of years, is Richie rich—one minute décor

Human can behave unjustified
But Lords are known to be just & fair, no malafied,
God's, please save children from—karmic cycle
Let them live happily till they grow and tackle.

The beautiful fresh flowers and buds!
Withering with unbearable heat & clamping of fingers,
The poor little boy along with his buds & flowers
Shrieking for attention before it dries or withers.

The passer by—please open your soulful eyes!
See the poor flower seller's plight,
Give him some solace, a smile or hug him tight
Or at least buy his flowers; he cheers this day & night.

Beautiful line—give the best to the world!
And the best will come back to you,
Love, help, save orphans from poverty God will bless you
With love, luck, peace, Truth, forever; no blues!

M.F. HUSSIAN—MASTERMIND OF MASTERPIECES

M F Hussian—mastermind of masterpiece
Iconoclast artist, at 95 rests at peace,
Born in 1915, bids adieu in twenty eleven
He glides over the clouds and rests in heaven.

The Picasso of India, well known as Fida
Immortal artist, he was pride of India,
Indian nationality but a worldly figure
Creative genius with eminent international stature.

Incredible person, painter, patriot, enthusiastic
Truthful, passionate artist in present and past,
One in hundred years will be Hussian
The whole countries, genre are his fans.

A modern man expressing modern art
His contribution is immense; he's done his part,
Created volumes of artistic dreams and muse
Gajgamini and Meenakshi[1] were truly his muse.

Hundreds of canvases, made movie on Madhuri's smile
God knows! Why he ended up in self imposed exile,
Artist, geniuses, should be understood well
Or we have to repent the loss and their farewell.

Fida—was a lover, dreamer of life
Bare footed, sanyasi, karamyogi[2] type,
Leaves an imprint on our mind and a legacy
Tons of work,—masterpieces-so classy.

---

[1] Gajgamini, Meenakshi: names of hussain's characters, heroines.
[2] Sanyasi, karamyogi: ascetic, monk.

At 95 of age he was active like a child
So humorous, energetic, excited, agile,
So romantic and fun loving in his red Ferrari
His passionate persona will empress our memory.

M F Hussian—a mentor to many budding artist
Tayeb Mehta, Jatin das, Anjoli Ila menon,
Praises and accolades for his undying spirits
His works of Art, value growing in digits.

An Indian at heart, wandering here and there
Be it Dubai, New York, Paris, London, Qatar,
Ambitious artist—truly a world citizen
God bless him—and his sole rest in heaven

PURSUIT FOR A VISIONARY AND MISSIONARY

All I need for my country is—a visionary.
Able statesmen, philanthropist, extraordinaire,
Charismatic, country man—Ideal
Rises our nations horizons, India—Shining and Ideal.

All I need for my country is a missionary
High ideals with noble character, booming bravery,
Zealous to the core, the utmost enthusiast
Dynamic camaraderie, ready for Herculean task.

All I need for my country is men of integrity
Soul of a Samaritan, heart ecstatic, full of dignity,
Country men with virtue, valour and vitality
Reliability like a Royal blood, boasting dependability.

All I need for my country is, mentor with morality
Mortals tend to be trapped in frivolous gamut of activity,
Men and Women flaunt their assets, flamboyance
Engage, indulge in futile desires of luxuries and affluence.

All I need for my country is a real leader
Yearning for learning, knowledge, voracious reader,
Gentlemen with grit and gusts, motto and courage
All countrymen—patriots—far above average.

All I need for my country is true democracy
India, nevertheless is a biggest successful democracy,
Portrayal of the people' for the people, by the people
This slogan should echo in all—strong and feeble.

All I need for my India—a Heuristic
Try try until you die; spirits—a realistic,
Explore every inch of creativity till Zenith—be holistic
Unique human being with an Aura—an Aesthetic.

WOMEN OF SUBSTANCE!

(Written on Women's Day)

God created Man—The Adam—miracle of humanity
Women—The Eve—Miss and Mystery of humanity,
Man and Women—two different entities with individuality
Made for each other, complementing one another's personality.

Man—a legend, icon visionary and magnanimous
Zealous, full of dignity, chivalrous and glorious,
Women—is precious, pure, full of compassion
Elegant, empowered with love, devotion and passion.

Women—truly, a women of substance
Soulful, sacrificing, stunning personality par excellence,
Successful, shining stars reaching the sublime
Spirited, charismatic and enchanting like an old wine.

Artists muse—A thing of beauty—joy forever
Designers fancy—damsels creating ripples over and over,
Flamboyant, fabulous, bold and beautiful
God amused by its own masterpiece—so wonderful.

Entrepreneur, astronaut, leader and super cops, path setter
Cool cultured, painter, doctor, or a life partner,
Politician, pilot, professional to the core
Or a coy, innocent, hard working home maker, girl next door.

The mesmerizing mermaid with curly locks
The labyrinth—the mystery of mistress flocks,
The mere glance with soulful eyes—wrecked sailors and ships
Bewitching beauty enhanced with lovely luscious lips.

Women in India worship men as Gods
Follow their path, unconditionally as lords,
Loves, hates, protects her man in accordance
Selfless sacrifice makes her—The women of substance.

Indian women is like Trinity
Creator, lover, preserver till eternity,
But if proved or harassed; becomes a destroyer
Eradicates the evils of society—a great survivor.

Women—The synonym for joy and happiness
The pivot, axis of man's world or business,
Around the world—women is revered
Loved and blessed; in India—she's worshiped!

Nirmal Rathore Bikaner

MILLION DOLLAR SMILE

(A Satire on Man Dominated Society)

God's been kind and benevolent to one and all
One gets beauty others brains, some great role,
Some get name, fame, pride, prestige and money
Million dollars few get, hug-you give honey!

Rich, famous and affluent are playing in crores
A house with ten rooms, many more tens of floors,
Family ties so fragile, locked in self cocoon and worry
Million dollars lots get, smile and hug they need honey!

Loneliness and unwanted feeling is the most bugging bug
Loads of luxuries, comforters, dying for love and hug,
Men and women competing with life's race
Million dollars earning, but, no time to dine-face to face!

Ego's, pride, attitude, kills the love and luck
Individual's stuck in identity clash, talks of muck,
Fight and argue on petty foibles and behave funny
Million dollars cannot replace—love and smile honey!

The master of house—The hubby thinks he's the boss
The queen of master—wife—the house holder at loss,
The hubby sacrifices leisure, fun, frolic at home
Wife balances by sacrificing self, don't compare honey!

Being boss of the house is O.K and acceptable
But bossing around on wife is intolerable,
Teaching and preaching of his family and his roots
Forgetting and neglecting—the wife's sudden uproots!

Two different families and culture, two personalities
Trying to yoke the relations, some become casualty,
Rather than solacing the buddy—who's home away from home
Mock her memories and worries—That's not fair honey!

In the realms of joy and success—don't be eccentric and callous
Love & praise your life partner—don't be zombie and jealous,
'Coz she's the toughest pillar of your life, honey
In the toughest struggle, failure, debt or money!

God bless the man dominated society
They think women are their personal property,
Blessing her with materialistic pleasures and million dollars
Forgetting love and The Million Dollar Smile—
The true treasure!

MARIONETTE OR MASTER OF MOBILES

(The present Generation Kids)

Human, wants to invent, explore and master
He likes to experiment and be a hard task master,
Be it language, studies and technologies
New visions, missions or new discoveries

The latest addition is the invention of mobiles
Man's best friend and foe, though very versatile,
It saves one's life, time, pride and labour
Yet doom's one's life, time, pride; neighbors envy.

Life after mobile phones is—pleasure and convenient
Human become more expressive and efficient,
Romance has doubled and doubled again
Sometimes romance vanished, love gone vain.

Today, the master of mobiles is its marionette
His soul hanging like a dagger, coz of net,
Career, courtship, life, wife—all its puppet
Dancing on the tunes of this monsters trumpet.

Think of the devil and the devil is there
Even if you are in the loo—he'll not spare,
He's the Boss, autocrat-nothing less than Hitler
Whether, like it or not, everyone owns it even the butler.

Life without mobiles is unconnected and unimaginable
It serves us like Ginni—anything, everything is possible,
World is connected in seconds, just by finger touch
Locally or globally, does marvels by mere touch.

The looks, features of this small wonder
Are pleasing and ever-changing shapes and colours,
Phone, photographing or video graphing,
A gadget, performing, messaging, e-mailing & programming.

The lovers, parents, bosses and dons
All can trace their buddies or loved ones,
Though playing like a puppet or marionette
Human is the master of mobile—You bet!

SOLDIERS TRYST WITH DESTINY

(Life in the Army–from dawn to dusk)

Life in the Army, they say is pretty fine.
From dawn to dusk—its different but truly divine
GC—gentlemen cadet to General-in-Chief.
It's a roller coaster ride with miracles, no mischief.

Handsome hunk with a crew cut, is the young officer
Heights of luxuries and paraphernalia—even a chauffeur,
Juniors are buddies, seniors followed as Gods
Duty unto death, come what may from lords.
The teenager turned 21, becomes an Iron man
Experiences new visions, missions and horizons,
Postings from Lalgarh to Warragte, Pattan to Andaman
No pity no remorse—Be a Man!
Lt, Capt—Major, Col—Brigadier, General
Life skips moments, months, years—unfathomable,
Son turns son of soil—the savior—charismatic and enthusiastic
Zealous to the core, with valour and vitality—so enigmatic.

Promotions, medals, awards are really inspiring
Seldom demotions, superseding proceeding disappointing,
The 7 is lucky number in normal routine life
9 pointer is desired, 7 the most unwanted in Army life.

Work is worship, nation always comes first
Command of orders—Yes Sir! is foremost,
Whether it's well or dungeon—rock or cliff
Soldier moves on—for an assault or a tiff.

Human beings are smart, over smart, forget being Human
Plays tricks and game, sometimes forget to be humane,
Men in uniform are steady as a stallion.
His love, luck, life is the Country, his own Battalion.

Life in the army—they say is pretty fine
Society has changed, seldom army men—lives on Border line,
Sweating in peace to avoid casualty in war
Competing with self, raising his own bar.

Life in the army—they say is pretty fine
From dawn to dusk, its different, but truly divine.

PRESENCE OF OMNIPRESENT

(God Is Here)

In the childhood phase, life was beautiful
Full of mischief's, blissful and beautiful,
In fathers eyes and emotions, felt—God is near
In mothers touch felt—God is here.

Adolescent age was exciting and challenging
Loads of discipline and duties, lots of zing,
While testing times, felt—God is near
In success and triumph, felt—God is here.

Youthful life rides on roller-coaster, at twenty five
Blessed with charming partner and child—Life truly live,
In spouse's eyes and promises, felt—God is near
In my child's eyes and innocence, felt—God is here

Life at forty is ambitious and dynamic
Paradoxes, mysteries, lucky yet nostalgic,
In peace, prayers and solace, felt—God is near
In miracles of destiny, felt—God is here.

The eventful journey of mankind—the real voyage
The fast and fabulous life—page after page,
In life's Chakravyuh[3]; the soul felt—God is near
In my child's dream and aspirations felt—God is here.

Today is the day to be lived and enjoyed fully
Live, love, forgive unconditionally,
In human blessings and benevolence, felt—God is near
In meditations and experiences, felt—God is here.

---

[3] Chakravyuh: maze, meandearing ways.

Divine life is amazing, in presence of omnipresent
Heavenly bliss—Atma[4], Parmatma[5]—Omnipotent,
In God's creations felt—God is near
Till eternity, God is the savior—God is here.

---

[4]   Atma: soul
[5]   Parmatma: God

HEROIC RAJPUT HEROINES

(Annals and antiquities of Rajasthan)

Rajasthan—the glowing state with valour and honour
The Princely states—The collection of kingdoms,
Rajput—'Son of King', literally the Raja Putra
Whose birth and traditional duty is ruling and fighting.

Heroism is in the blood of Rajput men or women
They live and die for commitment, pledge or vachan,
Though all human on earth are red blooded
But for Rajputs, by their Royal deeds—known as blue blooded.

Be it Marwar, Mewar, Shekhawati, Hadoti,[6] Chittor—
Be it Bikaner, Jodhpur, Jaisalmer, Jaipur, Kota—
Rajput princes—courageous, stories are endless
But heroic Rajput Rani's or heroines—are no less.

Colonel Tod's classic-Annals and Antiquities of Rajputana
Is testimonial to the courage, chivalry, honour of Rajputs,
Let me enthusiastically recount queens of Rajputs
Their pativrata, sativrata,[7] Johars or chopping the head.

'Padmini'—the queen of Mewar*—the incomparable beauty
'Allauddin's lust, reflection in mirror, an interesting story,
 She planned to rescue Maharana—riding on palanquins
'Coz of unfortunate defeat—courageously committed Johar.

The heroic Rajput heroines are endless
Haadi Rani of 'king of Salumber is unique example, nevertheless,
The newly bride—slicing off her head with sword
Sends it as souvenir—liberating her husband to fight fearlessly
      and bold.

---

[6]   Marwar, mewar . . . : states of rajasthan.
[7]   Pativrati, Sativrata: ideal wife devoted to husband.

Hundreds of amazing exemplary deeds
Of Heroes and Heroines of princely states,
Are heard and read with pride, since infancy
The tiny tots, teens are nurtured for tomorrow's emergency.

'Mira'—the princess of Rathore clan is exceptional courage
Married to Mewar king, but adorned Lord Krishna!
In orthodox days-she set on a devotional voyage
Leaving home, husband, Mira dedicated herself for God.

Sacrifice self for some great cause is bravery
Sacrificing self for honour and pride, needs courage,
Challenging norms and laws—need strength
The heroic Rajput Rani's—had them all in abundance!

AMATEUR TO CONNOISSEUR

(Artists progress from Zero to Hero)

Life is short, Art endures
The inspiration and expressions makes Amateur
The eclectic impressions and fascinations on canvas
The niche, the finesse transforms into connoisseur.

The passionate, vigorously exploring Artist
Striving his own strokes, resilient spirit,
Canvas of life transcends into surreal spaces
Consciousness in varied forms and faces.

Portraiture of vision, skills are divine
The vivid hues and colour—aesthetics sublime,
The palette, knife, brushes are his tool
On seventh heaven, in seventh sense is Mr Cool.

Picturesque landscape, serene seascape can muse
Portrait of deep eyes or smile can ignite and enthuse,
Inspire, and explore, every inch of creativity
Far from the maddening crowd and sensibility.

Artists can visualize beauty and illusion
Harmonies and synchronizes the eruption,
Vibrant kaleidoscope, soulful creations
Playing with zeal, feelings and emotions.

Artists are harbingers—reactive and proactive
Paints with ease, society;modern or primitive,
Artists studios—the Atelier, full of classy pieces
Faces, figure's—fabulous masterpieces.

Holding the brush and his breadth—the creator
Performs with magical fingers—as a meditator,
With heart and soul and undying spirits
Paints the whole world, cosmos—no limits

Satisfied completely, yet yearning ascetics
Anxious, energetic, romantic are Artists,
Creates priceless treasures, for generations
They are our pride and deserves felicitations.

Be it Picasso, Leonardo-da-vinci
Or MF-Hussain, Tyab Mehta or Anjolie,
All are geniuses—dreamers, excited art lovers
Metamorphosized from amateur to connoisseur.

Author with honorable Home Minister Shri Sushil Kumar Shinde

Nirmal Rathore Bikaner

THE DARK WORLD

(Inspired by Blind School visit)

At dawn the sun rises with orangish hue
The serenity and tranquility spreads all along the view,
The misty weather opens up, birds and animals open their eyes
But for unfortunate blinds—The dark world prevails.

The opening of rose buds or the sight of humming bee
Popping of poppies, blooming tulips teasing bumble bee,
Seeds sprouting, branching—becoming tree
But the unfortunate blind—The dark world prevails.

Newborn child, so tender and fragile, like flower, touch me not
His eyes like sunshine, smile so divine—oh God,
From teenager to adult, how time flied
But the unfortunate blind—The dark world prevail.

The journey of blinds is risky and challenging
For normal routine life—he's always striving,
Though with gifted senses he progress and succeeds in life
Proves better than the fortunate one's with eyes.

The dark sheep—the blot to society-the extremist
With nefarious plans to disintegrate the country,
The corrupt, heartless, shameless such men
Are more unfortunate than blind men.

Gods benevolence is unending and unconditional
All mortals are blessed with sound body and mind,
Few gifted people are doomed, due to karma[8]
For fortunate people, one should remember Dharma.[9]

---

[8]   Karma: own doings
[9]   Dharma: religion

Eyes are the mirror of soul
Expression of love, warmth, emotion, as a whole,
Undeserving genre should donate eyes
To the unfortunate blinds, brightening their dark world.

Lets all imagine for a minute—the darkness
The helpless, the scary, deadly loneliness,
Missing all creativity of God, nature, without eyes
Let's all pledge—to donate our beautiful both eyes.

APPLE—THE PROTAGONIST

God created Adam and Eve, also the Apple
The luscious Apple-for the first ever couple,
Allured Adam for a want, for a loving partner
Eve was created, both lived happily together.

Life was beautiful with a beloved lover
Adam without Eve, was pensive and a loner,
Apple—The protagonist played vital role
Adam and Eve cherished life as happy souls.

Once again, over the years—Apple was a hero!
Apple—the protagonist-awakened-great fellow
Newton—the great scientist, called out Eureka!
Discovered-gravitational force, called Eureka!

All inventions and discoveries are amazing
New ideas, new theories, gives life a zing,
Dropping of Apple was a mere coincidence
But for genius Newton, it was force-so evident.

Latest is the story of Steve Jobs Brand 'Apple'
Cared a damn to dogmas and tradition—created 'Apple',
His passion bordered madness with new pods
Various modes of I pads, I phones and I pods.

Steve Jobs was a restless, ruthless dreamer
Who converted and shaped into reality—his dreams,
Who dared to be different genre, felt the difference
He felt, life was limited, so live, enjoy the affluence.

Scientists, thinkers, researchers, technologist
Are born with unique inquisitive mind and logics,
Invention of 'Zero' by Aryabatta did wonder's
Dropping of Apple, though natural, did marvel!

The luscious Apple for Adam and Eve was amazing
Newton's Apple and Steve's Apple was challenging

Apple—The protagonist really played vital role.

100% PERCENTILE (CRAZY CUT OFF)

The adolescent's world is full of fun
Loads of nuisance, playfulness tons!
Mincing and munching pizza's, burger and buns
Playing video games, face book, instead of guns.

The monster of Board exams approaching
Adolescent is serious, sad and depressing,
House of midnight lamp burning
He wants to be successful, he's yearning!

The examination fever is over and out
No more fret, just dance and chill out,
Holidays, movies, masti; total freak out
Enjoy, entertain, indulge—till result is out.

Beware, Board results declared!
Gloom for some, boon for some who dared,
Above first division are millions
Perfect 100%, unbelievably; is just one.

This year, marks poured as cats and dogs
Above 95% was easy and desirable, parents blog,
The crazy cut offs were absurd and unrealistic
Students sulking, facing reality.

The toppers are lucky ones to flaunt
The intelligent and diligent, yet lot to mount,
The mediocre are plenty, no counts
For the defaulters—God save their souls' or they haunt.

The crazy cut off is worse than price hike
Every year rising high, touching the zenith,
From childhood the competitions are challenging
Human being suppressed by situations, is ailing.

This planet called Earth is rich and beautiful
This mortal called man is feeble and fearful,
Lord, give us love, light, strength and luck
We be triumphant; wish us-Best of Luck

WHEN WILL YOU BE HAPPY

Gods been kind and benevolent.
Blessed humans with love, selfless and talent,
Relations, power, character & personality
Gods foremost question to mortals-
 Oh Dear! When will you be happy

Tycoons, Industrialist, great business houses
The owners bestowed with luxuries, money oozes,
Lavish lifestyle, fleets of cars, jewels, still unhappy
Gods foremost question to tycoons-
Oh Dear! When will you be happy?

The intellectuals, genius and scientists
Teachers, Guru, Pundits and Artists,
All are great in their own field, unique personality
Gods formost question to brainy lot-
Oh Dear! When will you be happy?

The parents, grandparents, mother, father
Their kids rise high & higher, surpass others,
99 or 100 percent achievers, sulking & unhappy
Gods foremost question for parents-
Oh Dear! When will you be happy?

The soldier is a perfect balance of duty & devotion
He forgets his own life, sacrifices ambition & affection,
For valour & honour kills enemy, wants more; is unhappy
God's foremost question to soldiers-
 Oh Dear! When will you be happy?

The kids are blessed with Gods on earth
Their parents protect, earn for home & hearth,
Over abundance of love& caring, still unhappy
Gods foremost question to kids-
Oh Dear! When will you be happy?

THE GYPSIES

No house to dwell, no room to relax
No home, no kitchen, comforts, but shovel & axe,
Any place under the sun, they live & fire the furnace
And enjoys life-moving everyday to a new place.

No expectations from past, present & future
No tensions of home, hearth—live with nature,
A joint family with all working hands, smiling face
Yet enjoys life moving everyday at a new place.

No love, luck, lust for status, power or money
No complaints, no grudges, oh dear honey!
Life can be lived with satisfaction & slow pace
Like minstrels do, moving everyday to a new place

No friends, foes, relatives or competitors
Moves like sun, moving to directions to & fro,
Happy in their small world, no permanent base
Gypsies enjoy their solitude, moving to a new place.

No fashion, fusion in attires, no wardrobe
Their colourful clothes, self styled, no designers robe
Yet so unique, their hairstyle, dresses, & this race
Enjoys life to the fullest, though moving place to place

We the middle class, rich or aristocratic
Possess assets, riches for next generation-so majestic,
The more we attain, the more we crave
The Gypsies have none, yet enjoys-moving place to place

ENOUGH IS ENOUGH

From birth to death, childhood to adulthood
We live, grow from good to worse, or worse to good,
It's high time we realize or we say; oof
Enough is enough!

From truth to honesty or limits of dishonesty
Curb our selfishness, believe in integrity,
Stop our greedy ambitions; or we say oof
Enough is enough!

Rise above corruption, become an example
Live in satisfaction, where meager is ample,
Nation comes first; but errant defaulters ; oof
Wake up, Enough is enough!

Acceptance of unjust, wrong things, believe in tolerance
Is a bigger crime, ghastly as enemies alliance,
Injustice will prevail, spreading lawlessness—oof
Stop this complacence-enough is enough!

As children one loves to play and be jolly
Loads of fun, frolic, mischief's and be jolly,
Life's cycle teaches new lessons, new ways; oof
Child sometimes feels enough is enough!

As parents, we mature and nurture the kids
Loads of duties, responsibilities, as kids never did,
The children are bundle of joy; but sometimes,—oof
Parents regret, feels; enough is enough!

As politicians, elected by the people
Ought to work, for the people, of the people,
But occasionally one gets bogged down; oof
Common man, feels-enough is enough!
As mortals, the paradoxical planets effects greatly on us
Unknowingly in astrology-the sun, moon, Jupiter-make, mar us
As Guru's or Pandits views—Rahoo, Ketu ruins us-oof
It's a science or superstition; enough is enough.

NATURE'S WEDDING DAY AFFAIRS

When the dark clouds fly & the lightning seen here & there
When the rains approach with soft pitter patter,
The cool breeze blooms & mist romanticize the whole
    atmosphere
Red velvety bugs, mushrooms on the pathway-as if its
    nature's wedding day affair.

The flora & fauna bathed by rain droplets, so fresh
Contrasting flowers on trees peeping; playing hide seek,
The azure sky turning pale, orange, varied colure as—vibgyor
The rainbow appears suddenly, on the natures wedding day
    affair.

Colorful butterflies dancing like young damsels
Dressed with flamboyant ant motifs, in wedding ensemble,
Birds & peacock singing with their melodious flair
On the plush green lawns, for natures wedding day affair.

The sun God, on his chariot, as the bridegroom
Earth-the bride, decked beautifully with loads of buds & blooms,
The raindrops signaling the auspicious moments
Whole cosmos celebrating, natures wedding day affair.

The mortals too celebrating, as if in heaven
Thrilling, magical moments, wonderfully woven,
With trailing gowns & dresses, as brides maids
Invited specially for natures wedding day affair

At dawn—the dew drops, sparkle like pearls
Earth-the bride, adorns diamonds, and pearls,
Sun-the groom-most handsome shines brightest as ever
The newly wed bids adieu-at dusk; after the natures wedding day
    affair.

The fumes & perfumes of first rain on earth
Is as alluring & mesmerizing as first love, after birth,
Newly, wed's romance, tickling all senses, moods love affair
With amazing ambience, hues, on this ultimate nature's wedding
day affair.

DANCE OF DEMOCRACY!

Dance of democracy is divine!
In India, or anywhere in world, is truly sublime,
Freedom of speech, creates ripples or breaking news
Too much of freedom, ends in chaos & lawlessness.

Dance of democracy is divine!
The parliamentarians, the custodians of constitution
Ministers sometimes over react in frustration,
For the people, of the people, by the people-the motto
Governments rule the country, seldom-leave on auto.

Dance of democracy is divine!
The assembly works well, systematically,
Sometimes uproars & upheavals disturb North, South block,
Orators try their knack, wisdom and wit
Fuming and fumbling on opposition's wise tricks.

Dance of democracy is divine!
The ministers, chairpersons or workers of party
Loyalty and royalty shown, come what may; for party,
Prejudices and biases changing like TT ball
Create new alliances, new friends & foes in Heaven or Hell.

Dance of democracy is divine!
Lots of freedom, fundamental laws rights & power
Loads of constitutional power, money & muscle power,
Power corrupts and absolute power corrupts absolutely
The use & misuse of perks and amenities is likely.

The dance of democracy is divine!
The foreign, bilateral relations are flourishing & sublime,
Philosophy Machiavelli is on, Gandhian is turning obsolete
Non violence, co-operation strategy in tumultuous world
    is oblique.

Let the dance of democracy be truly divine
Let's live like friends, no foes—all fine,
Global world-with no army & no boundaries
Love thy neighbour, no whims & idiosyncrasies
Kalyug[10] be replaced by Satyug![11]

---

[10]   Kalyug: Iron age, Bad period.
[11]   Satyug: Golden period.

100-200 CRORE CLUB

India—the largest democracy in the world
With billions of people, rich-poor, young and old,
India shining in political & beauracratic speeches & logos.
Or in Bollywood—100-200 crore club, parties & promos.

Unity in diversity is scarcely seen every where
Be it caste, creed financial status, its rare,
The Richie rich of the country, rolling in money
The poor still struggling around poverty line, where is the money?

The politicians blessed with money, perks, and power
Few turn the apple cart in seconds, by muscle power,
Deals in 100-200 crore deals and projects
Becoming famous iconic by elections, adorning jackets.

The actor's super stars become God like
Their fans love, worship, imitate—actions in real life,
I wish if they could spare some bucks from 100 crore
For the salvage of their poor brother's woes.

From politics to bollywood or world of fashion
Mortals are spoilt by extravaganza, galore and fusion,
One rich man can save hundred poor orphans
One crore can settle hundred houses for slums
100—200 crore can create a whole new world.

If . . . .

LIVING BEYOND LIFE

In this mechanical world man goes on and on
From dawn to dusk life moves on and on,
Every sunshine brings rays of hope and wish to live
Every sunset gives a reason to hope for tomorrow,
     try hard and live.

Human body-the most advanced mechanism
Vital organs and parts, working in harmony—great system,
Every bit of our body part, functions are remarkable
Even the smallest finger or toe nail damage, makes us unable.

The heart—the life line of our existence
The brain, kidneys, liver, eyes equally give assistance,
The life force keeps the life going
But one can live beyond life by organ donating.

The heart transplant gives a new life
Impossible seems possible by doctor's knife,
Perceive the value of organs of man in coma
Donating organs to those, who face the trauma.

The two beautiful eyes, the mirror of heart
Living beyond life, by sacrificing self before one part,
Reliving, enjoying through others love and happiness
Let's become like God, live for others finish sorrowness.

Life, then will have no misery and tears
No trauma of losing our own near and dear's,
Life, full of enjoyment, fulfillment no depression
Everyday, a celebration of life, no frustration.

The life force keeps the life going
But one can live beyond life by organ donating.

OVER SWEETNESS TURN BITTER

Sweet sixteen is youthful, seventeen over sweet
Over sweet turns bitter, can't really cherish and eat,
Smart is awesome, inspiring and desirable
Over smart, if compared to is, laughable.

Being emotional and caring is good, but once it's over, it hurts
Think logically and analytically or you will cry in spurts,
Sharing others tragedy and situation is fine
But becoming culprit of catastrophe is, wasting time.

Confidence is an asset, but over confidence kills
Creates attitude—superiority or inferiority complex with all ills,
Confidence sails through all walks of life
Creates trust, well being, positivism no strife.

Passion and ambition are goals to fulfill
Sky is the limit, touch the zenith, take hurdles or uphill,
Over passionate person enjoys life, & its dreams
But over ambitious becomes casualty with unfulfilled aims.

Cool and casual is the happening, yeomen
Enjoying trivial bits of life's leisure, different specimen,
The meticulous and diligent create ripples
Exhibiting visions, now missions and miracles.

A well planned cuisine on platter is divine
Perfect combinations of delicacies to dine,
With ideal, taste, texture, colour and fumes
Even over doze of sweetness turn bitter like a bad perfume.

ALL IS WELL!

(Song of hope, bliss, love and luck)

All is well, or all is in the well
God alone knows, is India—a heaven or hell,
Life blooming or looming for love and luck.
Humans happy or sorrowful, leaving and living for buck.

All is well, or all is in the well
God alone knows, is Army—a paradise or place hard to dwell,
Soldier in ultimate Josh—chivalry and camaraderie
Or crushed by unfulfilled ambitions or reverie.

All is well, or all is in the well
God alone knows, in politics—daily promises to buy and sell,
The ministers, statesmen voted for brotherhood and peace
Some split parties in seconds, doom country in pieces.

All is well, or all is in the well
God alone knows, Youth—bliss or a dangerous bell,
The life line, sunshine of parents, bursting with energy
Powerful packages yet few misguided missiles, missing synergy.

All is well, or all is in the well
God alone knows, where is society heading? . . . . well,
Where is love, peace, purity and Anand?
Gone are the days of Teresa, Tagore and Vivekanand.

All is well, or all is in the well
God alone knows, where gyan and gyan-gurus are leading,
The value system, institution, true knowledge vanishing
Child, once was tender and innocent, now boss of house,
    spoilt by pampering.

All is well, or all will be well
God bless us on earth—a paradise, not hell,
Man—Let buds and flowers bloom to glory
Let Youth—take on, rise to zenith—with no worry.

All is well, Yes all is well!
God created man—man created heaven not hell,
By technologies and discoveries—anything and everything is
    possible.
Human Mind makes wonders, miracles.
Even the word impossible says—'I Am Possible'.

MISS CONGENIALITY

(Be Jack of all trades, rather Jill with bouquets and flowers)

Over the years, we've witnessed beauty pageants
Miss Universe, World, Miss India at endless events,
Miss Congeniality—is the need of the hour
Be Jack of all trades; rather Jill with bouquets and flowers.

Glowing complexion with shining hair is fine
The glamorous baroque embellishments are divine,
The luxurious brands with crazy advertisement
Splendid, sumptuous extravaganza affair are appeasement.

Jewellery enhances the beauty of brides and damsels
Cosmetic therapies, changes look and outlook of young dames,
Miss congeniality—is the need of the hour
Be jack of all trades—rather Jill with bouquets and flowers.

Elegance, confidence, dignity of work culture
Etiquettes, efficiency, grit and gusto—girl should nurture,
From dawn to dusk, around the world is our domain
Bless our planet with joy and happiness—Amen!

Being the mother, sister, daughter is fine
But be a friend, philosopher and guide, so divine,
Miss congeniality is the need of the hour
Be jack of all trades, rather Jill with bouquets and flowers.

Shoulder to shoulder—neck to neck is the competition
Be bold than beautiful, no blunders—repetition,
Be brave like a lioness, or the tigress
Stand tall like life's heroine, not mistress.

Life is tumultuous, tempestuous—extreme ups and downs
Lead the caravan, rather following the clowns,
Miss congeniality—is the need of the hour
Jack of all trades—rather Jill with bouquets and flowers.

Beauty with brains, profession or home's
Choose your dreams, missions, rise up to horizons,
Widen your vision, wisdom, try try and test
Miss congeniality is the need of the hour
Be jack of all trades, rather Jill with bouquets and flowers.

2011 FORMULA 1 FEVER

(Indian Grand Prix–Grand Finale)

India Shining—with new performances and experiences
Hosting common wealth games or formula 1 car races,
Be it glitz and grandeur of games of international hype
Or the spanking new Buddha circuit for high-octane
action one of its type.

The journey from Manesar to Greater Noida was
 great adventure
Two tickets two hours to go for opening,
Flag off-was impossible venture,
Traffic jams and red light were the real spoil sport
My F1 car was zooming at 120 prelude to F1 motor sport.

Mission impossible was achieved finally by flying speed
Delhi routes and roads were buzzing like million ants or bees,
As if our capital was raided and citizens fleeing and flying
Buddha International circuit was the spot-prime.

The chequered flag off, the cars-chariots of fire
The revving engines, deafening roars, burning track,
The daring champions-Vettle, Schumacher or Button
The gorgeous grid girls, rev up the glamour quotient.

The lineup for race-brands like Red Bull or Ferrari
Mc Laren, Mercedes, Terro Rorso or Force India,
The racing champions-Mark Webber, Alonso, Hamilton
The sole Indian hero-Narayan Kathikeyan.

The electrifying carnival atmosphere, gushed the adrenalin level
The zoom and vroom's of screeching tyres of dare devils,
The zig-zag circuit of 60 laps or 308 kilometers
Was echoed by cheers and claps, fuel uncounted liters

The team winning or losing were equally enthralled
The trophy—the grandest of grand pix in silver and gold,
The Metallica performance could have added the icing
But Lady Gaga's presence concluded the historic event—live.

India's shinning—with new generations and imagination
Super-sonic technologies and new inventions,
The latest craze or fever on Sunday-Grand finale
2011 Formula 1 life time experience of Indian grand Prix.

MUSIC FOR SOUL

(Inspired by Spic-Macay Evening)

Music is the food for soul
Mesmerizing and moving hearts, ultimate goal,
Renders peace, pleasure and tranquility
Music composers, lovers are holistic fraternity.

The instruments worshipped like Idols
They are blessed and rise as maestro or Icons,
The magical symphony, rhythm creates legends
Bestows accolades, kudos, praises at pageants.

Be it Guitar, Sitar, Veena, Tabla-all are divine
Peps up our hearts and soul, better than vodka or wine,
The sur, taal, riyaz[12] sours with high spirits
Preserves the heritage and culture in true sprits.

The Jugal-bandi[13] composition a splendid bonding
The synchronization is amazing spell bounding,
Mystical, magical lyrics, notes, beats and fingers
Expressions and innovations, blesses the singers.

Pt Bhimsen Joshi or Ustad Amzad Ali Khan
Pt Shiv Kumar, Zakir Hussain or AR Rahman,
Be it Asha, Usha or Lata Mangeskar-India's shaan
Youthful Sonu Nigam, Shankar Mahadeven or Shaan.

Internationally famous Cliff Richards, Michel Jackson
Madonna, Ricky Martin and John Elton,
Teenage throbs like-Beiber, Taylor, Miley
Ravishing rockstars—Shakira and Beyonce.

---

[12] Sur, Taal: rhythem
[13] Jugal-bandi: duet

The serene sensibility, melody and rhapsody
Surpasses all mundane activity till eternity,
The wings of blissful imagination unfurled
The reverie, dream world, fantasy unfold.

The musical bands like beetles and Boney-M
Backstreet Boys, linking park, Boy zone,
The Ghazals of Jagjeet-Chitra, Gulam Ali's
The great Gharanas[14] and the Baizu-Bawra's.

Music is food for soul
Mesmerizing and moving hearts-ultimate goal,
The Padma-Sri, Bhusans, Oscar's, Grammy's
Owners pride, truly neighbors envy.

---

[14] Gharanas: Brand

BLACK CAT COMMANDO's

(On Raising Day of NSG-National Security Guards)

When the going gets tough, the tough gets going
28 yrs of Raising Day-of Black Cats Commando's glowing,
The dashing, daring hero's fully armed and charged
Fast, furious and fabulous, swiftly barge.

On 16th October the thunderous sounds of guns and burst of
    tri-colour
Depicted the opening function of pride and Valour,
The thrilling hearts and thrilling sound of Helicopters
Enthusiastic Commando's, Slithering from Hepters

No remorse, no pity, no regrets
When NSG Commandos appear, no one frets,
He gives his strength and life, to spare ours
He sheds his blood and sweat to protect us.

The vigorous training and unpredictable battle operations
The surgical skills and precision, as doctor's Operations,
The brave hearts begin, when experts are done
He's the ultimate savior-The real triumphant.

"Sarvatra, Sarvoottam, Suraksha*" is the motto
He's brave than superman, gets praises and kudos.

The formidable strike force great visions and missions
    always abreast and agog
Rendering yeoman service, as buddies' never bogged,
Be it security, counter hijacking or hostage rescue
Bomb disposal, forensic experts with high IQ.

Raised in 1985 to neutralize the nefarious designs
Reckoned as—contingency best forces in the world,
Exhibiting professionalism and motivation to the core
Felicitations and congratulations Regional Hubs-four.

When the going gets tough, the tough gets going
28 yrs of Raising Day, of Black Cat Commando Glowing

Black-Cat Commando

MY EUROPE TOUR—BON VOYAGE

My flights of fantasy sours higher & higher
As I boarded the KLM airlines-great flier!
Arial view of Delhi city was awesome, amazing
Air hostesses serving with extravaganza & smiling.

Amsterdam-the first destination
Was dream come true, blissful, like a heaven,
 Raindrops rushing to reach us as mild drizzle
Complete ambiance was picture perfect, misty after the drizzle.

London, capital of united kingdom-the second destination
Much cherished & awaited for years; no less then heaven,
Euro star—train was a miracle of technology
Super fast, as an aircraft, meadows rarely enjoyed—an apology.

London eye, Big Ben, St Paul's cathedral & Buckingham palace
Brussels—Mannequin Piss, Belgiam carpets,
And the diamond factory-cut, clarity, colour, carat
Austria's—Atomiam and the photo shops.

Netherland or Holland's-Madoradam was marvelous
The amazing miniature replica of all the moments,
Vallendam-a dream village, with windmills & its natural beauty
One would surely change loyalty, to settle in this country.

The Rhine river cruises, I just can't forget
Was the most cherishing ride on water, you bet,
But Switzerland, Engelberg were truly Gods lands
On Mt Titles—the rotair ride was mesmerizing with lakes &
     ponds.

The snow covered Mt Titlis was spine chilling
We too played, threw snow, like berserk kids playing,
Loaded with woolens, still trembling & shivering
Posing with snow balls, endless-photo clicking.

Liechtenstein—the most beautiful smallest country
A sleepy little place with palaces, but no military,
A lesson for all mortals to live in peace
No boundaries, no enemies, just world peace.

DREAMS COME TRUE

The hopes, desires, aspiration and dreams!
Vary from individual-virtuous, great or lean,
Dreams are free for rich or poor—all is fine
Dreams comes true, just once or twice in a life time.

The kings & queens are like Gods!
Possessing all, still striving for more, so odd,
They are the blessed ones, still yearning for sublime
Dreams come true, just once or twice in a life time.

The soldiers are the pride of nation!
Lives for dignity, valour; Gods unique creation,
Lives & dies for duty, gets promotion with devotion
Dreams come true, just once or twice in a life time.

The politicians are the leaders, path setters!
Lead the country with matters of party, go getters,
They use or misuse fortunes—all is fine
Dreams come true, just once or twice in a life time.

The parents are the replica of God!
Pray, desire, aspire, dream for girls or boy,
Forget their own aspirations and ambitions
Strive, sacrifice for siblings-mission & vision.

Dreams come true, just once or twice in a life time.

Nirmal Rathore Bikaner

HOME SWEET HOME

The four walls create a house or building
Has all luxury, lots of rooms, floors, devoid of feeling,
The memories, the laughter, joys, sorrows shared bravely
A home sweet home, is where generations live happily.

The routine life sometimes makes home boring
Amusing resorts, foreign trips allure citizens frenzily,
Around the world, one goes with excitement
Home sweet home, is factually the final comment.

The grass looks greener on other side always,
A peep in others life, home, seems fantasy, anyways,
Anything looks beautiful from far of distance
Home sweet home, is the net result after varied instances.

After the days toil, in the gamut of activities
One is tired, squeezed of strength and energies,
One place on earth that welcomes you open armed
Is home sweet home, the abode-without harms.

Today's life style has some idiosyncrasies
Human drenched in selfish motives & sycophancy,
Faking, hiding, imitating for success, for self
Home sweet home, is the true place for true one self.

Every morn—the dawn is inspiring and challenging
New promises, new spirits, new dreams for fulfilling,
By evening, the dusk time—all mortals returns back
To home sweet home, the personal groove to dwell and deck.

All great things have an end somewhere
Kings, kingdoms, fathers forefathers leave us though so dear,
But the memories, foot prints are still intact
In our home sweet home, down the memory lane, in fact.

MY BRO—RAJYA VARDHAN RATHORE

My brother Rajya Vardhan Rathore, a Personality Par excellence
Hailing from Bikaner, Rajasthan—a thorough gentleman
   with benevolence,
A shooting star at Athens Olympic game
Won silver medal, rose to stardom and fame.

An Army personal, ace shooter—a debonair
Enigmatic icon, bravura, Idol, extra ordinaire,
Virtuous to the limit, yet warm and hospitable
A prodigy, heroic, well groomed and amiable

Gayetri—the better half is epitome of love
She's—a women of substance, gracious, bold & beautiful,
 Charismatic person, charming and convivial
A doctor by profession—still friend philosopher guide for all.

Manju aunty—a mother in true sense—so energetic
The pivot and quintessential pillar, so enthusiastic
An elegant, courteous lady, really workaholic,
Grooms the family with values, beliefs and ethics.

Manavaditya & Gauri are too precious gems
Flamboyant, friendly, fun loving still with great goals & aims,
Spirited to the core, focused, yet so humane
Kids of a celebrity, still so simple, untouched by fame.

My ten days stay at his home was a pleasant experience
Home away from home, with warmth & jubiliance,
On Raksha bandhan celebrated the ritual with full galore
Their love, caring and simplicity—I adore.

My utmost wish for this wonderful family
May God usher, prosperity, success and they live happily.

QUINTESSENTIAL FEATURES ARTISTS MUSE

A beautiful mysterious face, mischievous looks or smile
Catches the Artists fancy, he captures it alive,
The soulful expressive eyes, tender bow shaped luscious lips
Quintessential features of face, wrecked sailors and ships.

The nose so shapely and the long styled neck
The soft, charming complexion, without a speck,
Bewitching beauties, attract and invite the invaders
Bewildered they wander, even the crusaders.

The lock of hair, playing on the cheeks and chin
The onlooker, dying to touch the flying hair in wind,
The black beauty spot is the ultimate bliss
Doubles the glowing gorgeous gal's lips.

Face, features, when complemented by petite figure
Excitement quadruples, better and bigger,
'Nari'[15] wrapped in sari or multiple drapes
Enthuses artists heart, dressed in chiffon or crepes.

Jewellery adds on, to the regal poise and pride
Every beauty seems Divine like a Bride,
Tika[16], earrings, nathni, the necklace piece
Artist is blessed and portrays a master piece.

---

[15] Nari: Lady
[16] Tika, Nathni: ornaments

SALUTATIONS FOR XXII ON SILVER JUBILEE

(on 25ᵗʰ raising day of 22 Grenadiers)

Congratulations and Celebrations—Triumphant 22
The baptized baby in blood, our own double 2,
The bravest of brave, Bravo Brethren!
Most decorated paltan[17]—The Asoka Paltan.

1ˢᵗ June 88 The raising Day, was a day in History
Young stallions did wonders and miracles, created mystery
    and history,
Great men, martyrs—were daring, fought amazingly
With utmost grit gusto, heroism-become historic.

Team 22's—Good start was job half done
They lived and laid their lives, played with destiny and guns,
Baby turned—teenager, The indomitable and invincible team
From the valley of Kashmir, to far off Zaire, on UN mission.

Our family—son of soil, from top to bottom—toiled
Our General to Grenadier are, equally decorated and deserving,
From Ramendra to Kartar, the baton kept on changing
Smiling and Shining to glory, chasing and challenging
    Kargil heights—new milestones to zenith.

Rakesh, Vikram, Rajeev Joon, Jardeesh, Rajmal, Tej Singh
are iconic, enigmatic Brave sons
Duty unto Death, proved their motto, missions and mettle,
Gave us, the definition of heroism, conviction and gallant.
Made our-identity, The Bravest of Brave and The Ashoka Paltan.

---

17   Paltan: Unit

Watch your son at 21, twenty one, is a famous saying
Watch the son's of 22, twenty two, the fearless and fabulous-oh
    Boy!
Real Hero! RK Sharma, highest decorated, soldier,
With Kirti Chakra, Shaurya Chakra, and Sena Medal
Like phonics he rose, Param Veer Chakra yet awaited
Xavier Pillai a legend, our own Bravest of Brave,
    The most spirited solider!

The roll of Honour of 22 is great and unending
The citations, felicitations and awards, came rolling,
Today, 22 has turned 25, like a handsome Prince-with a legacy
    and harmonious team
The charismatic brave hearts, dashing with gallantry and fame

God bless our unit, with unity, integrity and honour
Camaraderie, Chivalry, Pride, Zeal, Zest and Valour,
We protect our belief, motto, values and Country
Remember and live up to the Credo-Naam,[18] Namak[19]
    and Nishan.[20]

My salutations to heroic 22, on silver jubilee.
My tribute to unsung heroes and their courageous deeds
My humble salutations to Veer Nari's[21]—The real Heroines
The mothers, wife's, daughters—on Silver Jubilee,
Their utmost sacrifice, support and motivation
Made these men, musketeers, great worriers and Heroes,
Long Live 22, Sarvada Shakti Shali[22], Long live India
Jai Hind!

---

[18] Naam: name
[19] Namak: salt
[20] Nishan: sign
[21] Veer Nari: Widow of martyr.
[22] Sarvada Saktishali: Bravo.

Nirmal Rathore Bikaner

ROSARY—REMINDER OF REALITY and SPIRITUALITY

Rosary the string of beads reminder of spirituality
Help me, focus on tranquility of reality,
Mind-like an untamed, reckless horse galloping
The poor little soul, seems distant and eloping.

Rosary the string of beads, reminder of spirituality
Teaches us—the Art of living and serenity,
Far from the maddening crowd—I tread
Materialistic world seems dream—I lead.

Rosary—the string of beads, reminder of spirituality
Close to my neck and heart, checks my sensibility,
Symbolic of Gods love, protects my soul
Reminds me of ambitions, successes and my goal.

Rosary—the string of beads, reminder of spirituality
In the midst of laughter or weird probability,
Like an anchor, saves the storm of voyage
Teaches me to forgive unconditionally and forget useless
    baggage.

Rosary—the string of beads, reminder of spirituality
Renders solace to bewildered, preaches maturity,
Man engulfed in fathomless pursuits
Endangers in frivolous ventures, seldom salutes.

Rosary—the string of beads reminder of spirituality
By meditation and prayers, rediscover own originality,
The divine experiences, atmosphere and enlightenment
The heavenly bliss till eternity and Destiny's miracles.

Rosary—the string of beads, reminder of Reality and Spirituality

CROSSING THE THRESHOLD

The security & sovereignty is our commitment
Be it self, society, country, no resentment,
Be the crossing of one's limit or the threshold
Or crossing the fences or boundaries, with hold.

Childs adamant demands or pampering is done
Competition or jealousy is fine, till its fun,
Excess of sugar, turns sour, so is the child spoilt
Crossing the threshold is a real jolt.

Teenagers life is momentary, on every day terms
Spends time, money, live lavishly, before he earns,
They are like misguided missiles, though full of will & energy
Crossing the threshold-is a fiasco-no synergy.

Adults too need to keep check on priorities
Curb their anxiety, no superiority or inferiority,
Live and behave gracefully, stay in own boot,
Crossing the threshold, is a big blunder; oops.

Countrymen ought to maintain nation's sovereignty
Spread love, brotherhood, harmony & purity,
Every nation nurture their heritage becomes tourist resort
Crossing the threshold-enjoy witnessing palace or fort.

All countries of the world, universe has one creator
The cosmos-life force created by God-the preserver
The natures, flora & fauna, animals and humans
     Crossing the threshold-no big deal-oh man.

All humans-a big family
Spreading love and tranquility,
No caste, creed or country.
No boundaries fences, frisking on entry
Crossing the threshold-no big deal-oh man.

INDIAN V/S NRI'S

Indians have a comparative, stress free life
The male genre dominant, looks after outdoor strife,
The ladies play important role, in indoor domain
The household job is shared by servants & maids.

NRI's generally lead a disciplined & busy life
No discrimination of workplace for husband & wife,
Both work hard—indoors and outdoors
Official, homely, personal agenda & many more.

Indians are some what orthodox & superstitious
Rituals, traditions, values are very precious,
Character & morals are their prime concern
They are the custodian of culture, legacy & clan.

NRI's have bonded, yoked Indian with modernization
Not really stuck with staunch views, no feminism,
Open mind with great outlook & visions
Professional to the core, great missions.

Indian women live like Queen
Endless comforts, luxury with high esteem,
She's the pivot of family, heart of the house
She's the quintessential person, lady of the house.

NRI' women are workaholic and busy
They are high tech, mechanized, never lazy,
She's smart, stern and sophisticated
She's independent, confident & charismatic.

Indian or non resident Indians
All have same heart soul & high aims.

DOCTORS DEDICATION

Doctors are like Gods-the great saviors
Daring, professional with dedicated behavior,
Sacrifices self, materialistic pleasures, leisure
Saves million lives; humanities treasure.

Doctors writing is illegible but God's wish
His spirit & vigour is ultimate, non selfish,
He looks so simple, does jobs so complex
His belief & vision saves mortals, doubts & perplex.

Be it physician or any specialist
Orthopedition, cardiologist or anesthetist,
Neurologist, pediatric, gynecologist
Doing his duties for God, as his priest.

The fatal ills & ailments bother humanity
Doctor serves with love, patience & humility,
Till the last hope, or the breath, he tries and hope
Does wonders with knives & scissors, wonderfully copes.

Every morn at 9 is the Doctors time
Even if he's awake till midnight, no time to dine,
Blessed with a smile, and a loving look
Dressed in sparkling white apron, walking gracefully with
    his book.

Being a doctor, engineer, pilot or astronaut
Is a dream of teenagers, few take this slot,
As a child, misses all the fun & frolic
Behaves mature, no mischief, turns workaholic.

Nirmal Rathore Bikaner

When difficult days loom, no hope in despair
When life comes to a standstill, intolerable to bear
On a robust stallion, rides this life saver
Does miracle's by mere touching his fingers,
    as Gods messenger.

Doctors are the shadows of Gods on earth
From life to death, & death to life and birth
He protects us with angelic looks & friendly hallo.
God bless this savior of mankind; blessed with a shining halo.

LOVE THY NEIGHBOUR

Love thy neighbour!
Despite the volatile relations or behavior,
They are close to your home, even if not to heart
Its destiny's choice, accept what so ever till you part.

Love thy neighbour!
In happier days, even if they didn't compromise or bother,
In catastrophe, even once if they cared & helped
They are God sent friends, to be tolerated
As a pinch of salt, gulped.

Love thy neighbour!
Be it any country, religion or society,
Exchange few smiles, gifts or pleasantries
Be nice and adjusting, even for the sake of formalities.

Love thy neighbour!
Be it Pakistan, China, who ever, what so ever,
If exchange gun fire, cross border nuisance and terrorism
Even when we are daggers drawn, tolerating extremism.

Love thy neighbour!
But for how long? How long can we be foolish, virtue less?
Injustice, over tolerance is a grave sin, not just vice
Tit for tat is the mantra of harmony & peace.

Love thy neighbour!
Is against animal Kingdom laws and obsolete phrase,
Survival of the fittest is motto, these days
Be it brother, friends or neighbour, all say.

Nirmal Rathore Bikaner

Love—we must our neighbour!
Create, healthy conducive, happy atmosphere,

Teach a lesson, where required, take appropriate measures
Transform him, as a good human being-life a pleasure.

Love thy neighbour!

PRIDE OF A BRIDE

Pride & panache of a newlywed bride
She's like a daughter, family's honour & pride,
Timid and coy, soft and sentimental
Beautiful looks with fabulous heart-so gentle.

A young little girl with dimples & sparkling eyes
Smiling & shining, tender heart, easily cries,
The pivot, centre of attraction, heart & soul of Ma
The life line, the true essence of love of Pa.
Grows without really knowing, so fast & hastily
The girl turns sixteen & then twenty one,
Parents heart starts beating; sinking now & then
The fears & feelings of farewell, troubles again & again.

The D-day approaches & the parents busy in arrangements
The daughter turns bride, with full embellishments & excitements,
The doll of the house; spreading happiness & fragrance
Marriage ceremony accomplishes with gay abundance.

The bride walks in, with pride & élan
Loads of blessings, tons of love, luck & shaan,
Lots of new relations, and great expectations
The doll turned bride, fulfills all desires & expectations.

The Pride & prejudices of a bride is unique
The code & conduct of the family also unique,
Maintains both families & houses traditions
Follows all rituals, values of all festivals.

The girl becomes bride and wife of one
Friend, philosopher guide for some,
Then mother-the foremost up gradation
Cherish the childhood play—the motherhood.

Pride & panache of a newlywed bride
She's like a daughter, families honour & Pride.

Nirmal Rathore Bikaner

MISSION POSSIBLE

(ought to be the motto of all Humans)

Mission impossible was a well known Hollywood film
Buts it's a disappointing, a depressive statement,
For brave hearts—nothing is impossible
Even the word itself say's—I'm possible.

Mission possible should be our motto of life
Struggle hard till last breadth, strive,
Clear vision, strong will power leads to success
Till zenith should be the ambition, horizon the access.

Mission possible ought to be the crux of life
High aims and aspirators, good decisions—well in time,
Every individual responsible for their bit
Any herculean job is possible, will be a hit.

Parliamentarians, leaders show helplessness
They have the power, but some misuse it, become shameless,
Policemen too has all power, but reacts late
Some are corrupt, some dedicated are slain, becomes late Mr.

Mission possible is aptly referred to scientist
From Missiles to Rockets to Agni, Akash,
They've proved their brains, mettle and enthusiasm
By trying Agni, Akash, Brahmoes and many more.

Mission possible is the key word for soldier
His life line starts and ends at mission, he never falters',
He's like God—made to win always and ever
Be at 1962, 65-71, Kargil war or any other.

Mission possible-starts with his confident—yes Sir!
What so ever be the hurdle or situation,
Be it difficult order—accepts with a sharp salute
Pride in his eyes, full Josh—always in yes Sir!

Mission possible—only possible with trust and faith
Only when you learn to obey—you can lead,
Only when you learn to listen—you can speak
And only when you learn to trust—you can win and succeed.

Mission possible only possible when you live for others
Live with humility, honesty, integrity for self,
Give the best to the world—and the best will come back to you
Try this once—and you will win the world.

Mission impossible is in the coward's vocabulary
For selfish, dejected, unbecoming human, devoid of bravery,
Mission possible should be our pledge today
Motivate every mortal, whatever mission comes our way.

3 MISTAKES FORCED ON RAJPUTS

(THE LOST REIGN)

Rajput—The royal and loyal blood of Rajputana
Led their life with pride honour and élan,
Rajputs played an integral role in wars and partition
Laid their lives for kingdom, country or realms.

I owe a debt of gratitude to my forefathers
A tribute to Royal legacy—the linage of great forefathers,
I am a proud princess of my own heart and soul
Enriched with values, valour, honour, great goals.

The history is full of brave moments of brave nobles
Examples and experience of strategies of war and wisdom,
The rise and fall of kingdoms—Prince and their whims
God save their souls for their blunders and fancy's.

Mortals can make mistakes—they are not God
Rajputs were made to do few foibles, blunders odd,
Excess of extravaganza, ruined their fate
They were forced to indulge in trivial pleasures
spoilt next generations luck fate.

In the prime time of their youth at eighteen
They fought for fatal wars—saka at sixteen,
But few were enamored and spoilt by luxuries
Mortgaged their kingdom, joined the enemies.

The bravest of braves second blunder or mistake
Few were fooled, boozed to glory—forgetting past glory
    for fun sake,
Once masters of kingdoms become slaves of frivolous ails
Once the blue blood some not even red became weak and pale.

The royal man with attributes of Hero
Dominated women as slave dynasty kept her under veil
    for long era,
Difficult rules, discipline, traditions and rituals to follow
Dominance proved to a disaster—system becomes hollow.

In Ramayan times—Sita had the right of swayamvar
In Mahabharat times; queens and princes had their say,
In Hindu culture—we never had veil system
Slave dynasty started this strange system.

Third mistake—the biggest blunder—was purdha system
It nullified all the great works of those times,
Women were kept indoors in veils for protection
But in the bargain—men were deprived of their wisdom
    and decision.

Even today if Rajput women get complete freedom like
    the erstwhile queen
The days are not far off when we can rule again,
With their supreme sincerity, loyalty and foresightedness
With honesty, integrity, we can rule the world.

WHEN THE HEART SKIPS A BEAT

At the dawn & dusk—the sunrise & sunset
The azure blue sky turns orangish, as horizon met,
The white clouds, cool breeze, engulfs the cozy surroundings
My heart skips a beat!

At the first tender touch of my child's cheek
The lazy yawn with sleepy eyes, so meek,
With the million dollar smile & shine in his eyes
My heart skips a beat!

On Mt Titlis, rising higher & higher, on rotaire
The tall showy peaks, the breathtaking nature's flair,
The chilling breeze with shivering lips & fingers
My heart skips a beat!

On the marriage day with full paraphernalia
When daughters decked as bride, also the complete galleria,
With last longing looks & teary expressive eyes
My heart skips a beat!

When the beloved, looks back with amorous glance
Just by looking in the eyes of loving fiancé,
The heart starts beating faster & faster
Suddenly my heart skips a beat.

When the buds blooms & the petals fall
By the tender touch of butterflies wings, and winds, spreading
    fragrance all,
When the baby birdies, try to fly
My heart skips a beat!

When life partner is away for long, when the loneliness becomes
    intolerable love forlorn,
With the first glance, the touch of caring arms
My heart skips a beat!

FAR FROM THE MADDENING CROWD

Far from the maddening crowd!
Serene seascapes, landscapes innumerable flying clouds,
Where butterflies dance on nightingales' song
The horizon, where earth & sky meets, the heart & soul along.

Far from the maddening crowd!
Harmony & peace dwells, no noise aloud,
Where cool fresh breeze blows, spreading fumes & fragrance
Tranquility and serenity over flows; sheer magnificence.

Far from the maddening crowd!
Where mortals live an enlightened and awakened life,
Away from the materialistic world
In harmony are heart & soul and spiritual life.

Far from the maddening crowd!
Bliss & happiness hugging each other, feeling proud,
 A world without woes & sorrows—we dream
No mischief, no malice our foremost aim.

Far from the maddening crowd!
A youth, full of joy & laughter never bowed,
Accept all challenges & adventures smilingly
Full of confidence, no regret, lives daringly.

Far from the maddening crowd!
A world with no hurry & worry, no noise,
No old age, ailments, no pain, no helpless
We live, smile, enjoy, like a child, fun loving & carless.

Far from the maddening crowd
I yearn, leap for such beautiful world.

Nirmal Rathore Bikaner

TURN A NEW PAGE IN SOMEONE'S LIFE!

Living for self, enjoying and cherishing moments is routine
Living for; fun, eat, drink and be merry, relishing different cuisine
Live differently—for others-worth for friend or wife,
Try your bit—give the best efforts and strive
Turn a new page in someone's life!

Giving a smile, hug or a helping hand to one
Gives you loads of happiness, contentment and fun
Unexpected love, caring or financially by money,
Gives solace to soul and blessings—O honey
Turn a new page in some one's life!

A lonely little boy, or a deserted dame
Life's struggle with destiny, achieve high aims
The ailing mother of someone or frailing father of one,
You become the savior—his destiny, his God
Turn a new page in someone's life!

A sports person dying to perform for country
Sweats day and night, forces the limits of his body
For years he struggles and slogs for a slot,
But unfortunately, he's oblivion, he flops
Turn a new page in someone's life!

Tons of Richie rich, their brats bored by school books
Involved in social networking, turns—robotic fools
No passion or emotion, no hurry, worry, no commitment,
But for destiny's child—he's a scholar—wants to rule the
    continent
Turn a new page in someone's life!

The gender bias is unimaginable awkward
Heinous crimes on tender girls, humanity going backward
Low morals, abduction, molestation or prostitution,
Women succumb to their ill fate; where is constitution?
Turn a new page in someone's Life!

Life is a cycle—a toddler, teenager, adolescent adult and old age
Every stage, having its fun and beauty—eventually pilgrimage
Loving toddler, tantrums of teenager, adult matured morally,
Old age is most challenging—physically and emotionally
Turn a new page in someone's life!

The more I understand human beings the more I love animals
With ego, lust, greed, jealousy, human being suffer,
With selfless loyalty, unconditionally animals love us
Turn a new page in someone's life!

SNAKES and LADDERS

(Symbolic of today's Life system–fair, unfair game)

Snakes and ladders is an age old kids game.
It's symbolic of today's life system—fair, unfair game.

When the going gets tough, the tough gets going
The royalty and loyalty works well with real Heroes,
Selfish minds stoop down for success, are zombies and zeros.

Men with courage live with conscience and conviction
Work with integrity, determination and dedication,
Cowards work for gratification and materialistic pleasure
Ladders of success comes to those, who value true treasure.

Snakes and Ladders is an age old kids game
The lucky ones are blessed with instant ladder and fame,
The vicious black sheep's are smitten and bitten by snakes
Though few times their chicanery sells like hot cakes.

Life teaches us to be truthful human—play fair game
Live and let live happily, honestly—earn good name,
Some defaulters, defunk and derail value system
Some offenders surreptitiously climb the ladder, defame the
    system.

Intellectuals, geniuses toils for years in oblivion
Sports personalities perform and move to pavilion,
Soldiers bleed in peace to avoid blood in war.
Snakes and ladder be bestowed fairly—is the need of the hour.

Human ought to rise from callousness and slumber
Learn from animal kingdom to be survivor,
Survival of the fittest is the rule of the game!
Tit for tat, strongest devours weakling—leads to food chain.

Snakes and ladders is an age old kids game.
It's truly symbolic of today's life system—Let there be fair game.

Nirmal Rathore Bikaner

FREEDOM IS MY BIRTH RIGHT

(VOICE OF WOMEN)

Freedom is my birthright—I will achieve it!
With, will power, determination and grit—believe it!
Break the barriers and shackles of—so called society
I am a free soul, a free bird, no one's proprietary.

Freedom is my birthright—I will achieve it!
From pseudo bondages and relations—relieve it!
Fake smiles, love! Miles away—Just pretence
I firmly detest the power of dominance.

Freedom is my birthright—I will achieve it!
Sweep the deteriorating system and hierarchy—finish it!
Destroy the decimation between caste and class
Eradicate from mother Earth—the evils, callousness and crass.

Freedom is my birthright—I will achieve it!
Break all superstitions faulty rituals—ban it!
Sacrificing self for the sake of, so called loved ones
Flattering the fools, foes, bosses or dons.

Freedom is my birthright—I will achieve it!
I will dream big, think big—witness it!
Cherishing and materializing visions and missions
Touch the Zenith, keep all promises.

Freedom is my birthright—I will achieve it!
Free myself from emotional, physical, financial bit,
No heart breaks and rolling perpetual tears and fears damn it!
For deceitful dudes, fake friends—near and dears ones.

Freedom is my birthright—I will achieve it!
Free myself from moral policing and moral duties—mind it!
I'll enjoy my birth, identity, brains and beauty
Celebrate my life's emotions, passion—enough of tragedy.

Freedom is my birthright—I will achieve it!
Abolish the man dominated society—ban it!
Born to a women! Man tries to bully his creator!
The mother, life partner, daughter or sister.

Freedom is my birthright—I will achieve it!
Punish the brutal torture and tormentors—believe it!
But love the loving, caring deserving ones
Forgive the defaulters who regret their faults and fortunes
Freedom is my Birth right—I will achieve it.

OBAMA V/S OSAMA

(US President v/s chief of Al Qaeda)

What is there in a Name?
Said Shakespeare, poet of world fame,
Obama, Osama juxtaposition just by one syllable
Confusion, contrast created such by one letter or syllable.

Obama—The new president of America
Enthralled were Americans, called out—Eureka,
New horizons, new hopes new motto—'Yes We Can'
Portrays a young, confident charismatic President.

Obama, the young blood, ambitions to perform
Completes one year, still firm and in full form,
Travelled, around the world in some dollars
Treaties, policies, collaborations in white collars.

The 'decisive blow', closing chapter of Osama
Bin—laden killed by US Seals, ordered by Obama
Oh lord! what confusion—Obama /Osama,
One letter difference creates—mania
Oba-mania or Osa-mania.

Osama killed—relieved one and all
The rise of Obama, saves his fall,
God delete and erase all negative database
Cut, copy paste all positive face.

This world should gain its glory
Love, peace, happiness, good memory,
Tranquility, serenity and dew spread meadows
A child's dream world—Heavens shadow.

A perfect life, better than imagination
Fantasy, flowers and blooms, fascination,
Human so humane, like deities; God
Help us—men and women 'oh dear lord'.

Nirmal Rathore Bikaner

FORLORN LITTLE SHEPHERDESS

(On the barren lands)

Life is beautiful for some, but hazardous for some
Luxury unlimited for some, utterly limited for some,
Yesterday I witnessed a pretty little shepherdess
Casual carefree looks and attire but a conscious worker.

Her tender age, demanded a home and a school
She deserved a loving family, love, care, fun,
But the forlorn shepherdess holding a slender stick
To manage her cows and goats on a lonely road side.

Unknown by her past future, busy in her present
Oblivion of lives treasures and pleasures, sun, moon, or
    crescent,
No dreams, desires, demands at all
She's unnoticed to the world—rearing animals.

Such life is pitiful, why is she a destiny's child
But her life is with no hurry's worries, no doubt
She's completely happy with God's little blessings I bet!

If I compare anyone's life with hers
We might be blessed with luxuries and comforts more
But happiness, thankfulness, carefree—she's got more.
She's the most satisfied human being than us

Her youthful red cheeks and the rosy lips
Her flowing locks playing on her chubby cheeks,
Her mismatched colourful cloths were like
Modern designers trendy outfits with tatters.

Children are like buds, tender and fragile
They bloom with love and caring turn active and agile,
Their eyes should see dream of tomorrow
As today may be our, theirs is tomorrow.

That forlorn little sheepherders
Drew my attention and imagination to wonder,
Tons of children are deprived of their luck
They mature before their age, society sucks.

Lets learn from this forlorn little shepherdess
To live as Gods gives—with dignity,
Never to complain worry or ask for
Let God's blessing shower on every deserted forlorn!

MAN & WOMEN—IMPERFECT MATCH

Man and women—two different entities two poles
Sometimes attract or repulse, as north and south poles,
With completely different countenance, heart and soul
Nature, behavior, habits, hobbies and goal.

Man—is rough and tough, hard nut to crack
But in love-adore, allure and sympathies has a knack,
Half the times fooling or living in fool's paradise
Impulsive, reckless, dying to be wealthy and wise.

Women—is petite and dainty, but mentally robust
Always in unfathomed love—sacrifices self, no fuss,
Leaves her own home, name fame, identity—for one
Who rides her on horses, few leaves in a lurch for some-one.

Man boast of bravery, chivalry and daring
After few years, love vanishes for dearest darling,
The oaths and vows seem trivial formality
Forgets the amorous looks & love, better half's responsibility.

Women, thy name is vanity—the better half
Seldom frivolous and unfaithful; never bitter half,
Sheds tears in solitude, yet man's strongest strength
Tries to adjust, to discover, redefine her own wave length.

Man, women completely different, yet complement each other
They are happy, when they live, bond together,
Little sensibility and less of expectations
Can save the situation of rocking relations.

Man O, man—love your lover and express it
'Coz in true life—speech is golden, silence—damns it,
Women, dear—accept with grace and gratitude
Just remember true love, forget ills and attitude.

Adam and Eve-were actually the perfect match
We too can try to be Adam and Eve—a perfect match!

Nirmal Rathore Bikaner

BLESSED WITH BOYS YET YEARN FOR A DAUGHTER

(Written on Karvachouth)

A loving life partner, romantic and royal
Dedicated soldier, handsome and loyal,
My life is full of blessings, happiness and laughter
Blessed with boys, yet yearn for a daughter.

The days in and out has gamut of activities
Being a versatile artist, busy in creativities,
Some lonely moments in the midst of laughter
I feel, I am blessed with boys, yet yearn for a daughter.

The household, interiors or outings
Lacks feminine touch, clash of likings,
The cuisine, talk over dining table and laughter
I know I am blessed with boys, yet yearn for daughter.

The spirit of shopping and the enjoyable bargaining
The selection of diamonds, jewelry or dress designing,
My deep desire, crush under brat's laughter
I am blessed with boys, yet yearn for a daughter.

The passion, emotions, feelings and sentiments
Suffocates, sometimes in futile male arguments,
I am a strong personality, and enjoy laughter
I am happy blessed with boys, yet yearn for a daughter

Teenage boys are difficult to tame and handle
God knows, how on earth, I could have managed girls,
No tensions, no sinking hearts, just laughter
Thank God, I am blessed with boys, yet yearn for a daughter.

Wedding planners, designers and caterers
Are the most envied for their fancy pleasures,
Girls wedding is a great mission, full of tears and laughter
I am blessed with boy's sometimes I wish I had a daughter

Today is enjoyable, but tomorrow will be satisfying
Maturing with grey hair and new relations tying,
Be it boy or girl-should have respect for mother and father
I am blessed with sons, their wife's will be our daughters.

Nirmal Rathore Bikaner

AROUND THE WORLD JUST BY A CLICK

Around the world in eight dollars was an old film
Today we can go around the world by just a click,
The technologies so advanced by computer age
Get connected to the world, networking with supersonic pace.

A different life with global revelations
Sky is the limit knowledge with no limitations,
Endless books, encyclopedias, libraries unfurled
Fathomless store house of data and information's told.

Every feature of computer man made magical machine is unique
The different software, programmes are fast and quick,
The little jinni performing, orders of master
Be it day-night or throughout day and night faster than master.

By internet-one gets connected in minutes
Exchange anything and everything, no gimmick,
From photographs, documents or love letter
With least of effort, job done ten times better.

Just by one click, we can do wonders
A miracle happens just with a click, one ponders,
Around the world, we can see and visualize
Learn about the mystery and culture, before one realize.

The communication for loved ones is awesome
The feelings, sentiments seen, read, felt by everyone,
Distances have no hindrance, no matter
Relations and friendship maintained—better.

The computer, laptop, iphone or ipad
Is like a vital organ, not just a fad,
It saves energy, time, life sometimes
It's a marvelous miracle-one of its kind!

TEENAGERS TEENACHE

Sweet sixteen is symbolic of most lovable, adorable stage
Fifteen is under sweet & seventeen as over sweet age,
The youth—full of vigour and exuberance
Laughter, mauj & masti, mischief in abundance.

Teenager's life revolves around friendship net
Before their eyes open, they open face book on net,
Posing, clicking, loading, downloading their smart faces
    with smart phones
Exchanging funny text messages & mails since morn.

Teenager's day is full of fun frolic & jubilation
Enjoys every bit & piece of life, full celebrations,
Smiles, grins, laugh to glory, lives joyfully everyday
Loves every moment, as if it's the last day of holiday.

But the smiles & laughs turn suddenly in teen aches
The balloon bursts, and the scenario complete changes,
The rivalry, jealousy turns friends into foes with heart burns
Teenager behaves whimsical with all tantrums.

The teenager's experience, a new lesson everyday on life
New friends, new peer group, pressures to strive,
The classmate, roommates seems perfect as soul mates
Teenagers teen ache troubles as destiny or fate.

REALM OF RHETORICS

Living in fool's paradise, Realm of rhetoric's
High ideals and expectations but blessed by anti climax
Speech is silvery, silence golden—is an old cliché.

Man tries to talk big, but live in a cozy cocoon
Stereotyped success, love, and life, few reached moon,
Man tries to impress by demeanor and outlook
Exaggeration, hyperbole, similes from the book.

Some flaunt their beauty and bodies, some brains
Few boast of genius, intelligence in vain,
Choicest few have all the muscle and money power
Seldom thinks of other soul's—just building high towers.

The tycoons, bureaucrats, politicians play game
Do wonders, blunders for just name and fame,
Whom does a common man complain
The innocent is crushed, his destiny blamed.

Boss is always right—is the thumb rule No 1.
If boss is wrong refer rule No.1, just enjoy the pun,
For bonuses and promotions people crave
But martyr live and die for nations are brave.

The widow of martyr, his mother and fathers
God alone knows the miseries that follows,
They show a brave brazen face, holding tears
They are completely broken, but hide the fears.

The child in the womb is shaken to spine and cells
The commotion inside creates—alarming bells,
The infant's birth regulates theory of evolution
We must progress, develop a cordial civilization.

From dawn to dusk, sun rises and sets
Moon and stars twinkling to glory and zest,
Man! Wake up from fool's paradise—Realm of Rhetoric's
Lead our destiny out of Armageddon—Life so classy.

BEAUTY PAGEANT

(Inspired by trip to Emporia and Promenade)

Beauty pageants are extravagant spectacle
Miss India, World, Miss Universe-International,
Beauty lies in the eyes of beholder
Epitome of panache, heads high and higher shoulders.

The Goddess of Beauty and Fashion
Bewitched by glamour' ambition and passion,
Shoppers stops, Pantaloons styles and trends
This damsel making lots of foes and friends.

Face masked, patched with foundations and concealers
Lipsticks, Eye shadows, mascara and blushers,
Simple dame-transformed into a goddess
Her own heart and soul fails to recognize.

The ramp, the walk—the attitude
Living in crowd but truly—in solitude,
The gorgeous elegance with flamboyance
The grandeur, luxury and affluence.

The attire, jewellery and accessories
Mesmerizes fully, with little worries,
The magnificent décor, amazing ambience
The fabulous looks, Indulgence par-excellence!

On the D day—the final steps and the glowing face
The confidence, demeanor, quintessence of Grace,
Penultimate attitude-panegyric answers
Bestows crown, flowers and tears.

Professionals bless and thank their stars
Creates a regal queen—a shining star,
Beauty queen waving, felicitating flaunting to the crowds,
The curtain falls, still cheering crowds.

The glamour, grandeur, cosmopolitan icon
The diva sashayed, shimmering elan,
Beauty pageants are extravagant-spectacle
Miss India, Miss world, Universe, international.

THIN LINE OF DEMARCATION

There's a saying which says—
There's a thin line of demarcation
Between a genius and insane,
Also there's thin line of demarcation
Between ego, attitude and self respect of person,

To stay happy, peaceful and with satisfaction
No love lost, no friend, foe and expectation
Live life in moments, before it becomes memory
Live to the brim of life's goblet, before it becomes history

Day and night, two phases of time
Joys and sorrows two emotions of mankind
Life's moving on and on—evolution,
There's wide difference of demarcation
Who enjoyed and lived or who lost and regretted.

Over sweetness turns sour or bitter
Over infatuation or love turns into jitters,
Over protection and pampering makes a recluse
No one can calm or soothe, unless self rescue.

There's a thin line of demarcation
Between love—hate affairs and relations,
The best of best friend, turns worst enemy
The most sacred relation, rocking on the rock, believe me!

There's a thin line of demarcation
Between honesty, integrity and corruption
To save our souls or dear ones abduction,
The theory of Animal kingdom persists
Live and let live, the survival of fittest!

Don't ask for too much, believe in satiation
Live life on daily basics, no regrets, no hesitation
Smile and laugh whenever get a chance
Life's incredible, precious, never get second chance!
There's thin line of demarcation between life and death
So live to the fullest, realize its value and worth

Nirmal Rathore Bikaner

ECSTASY & CATHARSIS

From a tender bud to a blooming flower is ecstasy
From a stream, river to ocean is ecstasy,
The wings of freedom and dreams, is fantasy
My aim of ideal happy world—utopia, is fantasy.

Ecstasy is azure sky, with crazy clouds varying
Amidst the majestic mountains, let me scream loud,
Feel and hear the echo—again, again and again
Experience the silence of nature, enjoy life once again.

The vibrant vibgyor colours of rainbow
The picturesque and psychedelic, under water fishes—oh!
Ecstasy I feel around waterfalls, fauna and flora
Ecstasy I feel in God's meditation and aura.

The pure and beautiful may face catharsis
The loyal and loving may be devoid of bliss,
The rich and flamboyant blessed with love and luck
The poor and starving, poverty ready to suck.

The discrimination kills all communities and nations
The disintegration, fractions ruins the nation,
This world stepping down with greed and phobia
 This world shrinking, human, feel claustrophobia.

How long can we live in illusion and idiosyncrasies
Just be pleased by innovations and discoveries,
Let's give our kids—a happy world and loving memories
Bless ourselves with Heavenly bliss and soulful victories.

Let flowers bloom and children smile, and flourish
Let the rain drops tickle us—we enjoy and cherish,
Let sun and moon shine in glory and ecstasy
My aim of ideal world—Utopia

"A reality not just fantasy"

TRYST WITH DESTINY

(Experiences Unlimited from five to fifty)

Tryst with destiny is life's experience
Great scenario—wonders and brilliance,
Joy, happiness, luck, luxuries abundance
Living life leisurely, at our own convenience.

On the travelogues' onset, was the embryonic phase
The tender heart, small dreams with innocence,
The cynosure, blue eyed of dear ones
Life revolving—I, me, myself, only attraction.

Teenagers phase with tens of frolic and fun
Imitating parents, teachers in sari's and buns,
Endless reveries and fantasies, talks and gossips
Tom boyish debonair, imagination; no logics.

Life at thirties and forties was the real pursuit
Of career, excellence, stability and spirituality,
Competition—neck to neck, thrilling, no relief
Dilemma's, decisions, paradoxes and belief.

Half a century at fifty, will be some achievement
One handsome hubby two brats, management,
Yearning for learning—trying all talents
As—artist poet, lecturer, also glider pilot.

Riding the horses performing jumps and stunts
Shooting the bull's eye—by pistols and guns,
Golfing and para sailing, once in a while
Daily meditations, yoga and walking a mile.

The exploring of artist is most cherishing
Sky is the limit—art, amazing and challenging,
The spectrum of colours, hues on the pallet
Imagination, realism as varied taste and palate.

The driving zeal and zest of driving venture
The spunk and chutzpah and adventure,
Driving cross country—Kashmir to Kanya Kumari
Life time experience of—"Women Car rally".

Poets introduction, and rendezvous is Pristine
Bombardic ideas, emotions and passions—divine,
Tryst with destiny—is my life experience
Great scenario—wonders and brilliance.

COMEDY OF GENERATIONS

(Reality check of our latest gen-X)

Comedy of generations is interesting indeed
Nostalgic of yester years and heroic deeds,
Grand fathers, great grand father's life
Better, bountiful, eventful with lots of wife.

Once upon a time, they were happy with sun, moon, stars
Today men has reached moon; on earth are stars,
In past people were blessed with hundred sons
Today's tragedy we generally have one.

Today-the children are innocent till seven
Wish to flaunt their body and wits at eleven,
Sweet sixteen is most vulnerable and eventful
They think they are Einstein—parents are fools

The looks, attire, behaviour has gone for a six
They decide their own destiny, marriages fix,
Some are angels, but few are devilish
Some are divine, but few doomed and selfish.

Old is gold, valuable as is old wine
The oldies, old songs, growing gracious with time,
The fantasies of youth is charming and fine
The successful generations, no time to dine.

The Ma's or grand Ma's food was delicious
The recipes and cuisine of sis is sumptuous
But for the generation 'X' there's a question mark?
Who's going to cook! Ms or Mr Marc?

The Gender blender and the freedom of thoughts
has confused our kids, to decide their slots,
Husband and wife rarely compatible
relations and bondage like bubbles, seldom comfortable,
Comedy of generation is interesting indeed
Nostalgic of yester years and heroic deeds.

INDIRA—
INDIA'S IRON LADY

Indira Gandhi-India's Iron lady
First women Prime Minister, most charismatic leader,
Leading one of the biggest democracy of sovereign India
Ruling for longest terms of ten and four years.

Symbol of India's indomitable spirit
Her political tenacity, formidable reputation of
great statesman,
Had an aura of power, a forceful spokes women
Rode a wave of success with India's victory over Pakistan.

The only daughter of Jawaharlal and Kamala Nehru
Studied at prestigious Somerville College—Oxford,
Joined Indian national congress, married Feroz Gandhi
Blessed with two sons Sanjay and Rajiv Gandhi.

At 12, she headed Monkey Brigade and moved on and on
President of youth Congress, Minister of Broadcasting
    and Information,
Finally in 1966, she become The Prime Minister
Earned a reputation of a shrewd and tough politician.

Her vision of developing vibrant India by will and commitment
Strengthen the nation of freedom and its achievements,
Lead lots of campaigns, missions, elections, by elections
Strong personality superb selection, ruled our nation.

The first lady Prime Minister did her bit
Conquered hearts, still-assassinated by her own guards hit,
All great people face criticism and resignations, one wonders!
Assault on Golden Temple turned out to be her biggest
blunder!

Indira Gandhi, India's Iron lady, so Charismatic
Great persona, personality so different and enigmatic
Leading a nation for fourteen years, not a easy cake
Live example for women to rise above, for women's sake,

Nirmal Rathore Bikaner

HINDUSTAN & PAKISTAN

The abode of Hindu's is Hindustan!
And the homes of Muslims is Pakistan?
I strongly oppose this discrimination
We'll unite them one day is my determination.

The God's have not created Caste Creed and Nations
Let's not disintegrate into new formations,
Let's try all permutations and combinations
To discover Win—Win situation and jubilations.

The face, colors, hearts, soul and blood
Is of all Hindu's and Muslims same; you dud,
The deities are same, just with different names
As flowers which bloom with different fames.

Man! why can't we rise above self?
As bible says "Love thy neighbor like thyself",
Hitler, Saddam, Gaddaffi, Osama are doomed
We the sacred souls are cheated and fooled.

Down the memory lane—I tread
Hundred of heroes, champions who lead,
A united Hindustan, brothers in arms
Today—divided we stand, fighting with arms.

Technology and discoveries better than past
Generation 'X' is heart less, though super fast,
Lost all love, brotherhood or tolerance
Generating wars, hatred, greed and nuisance.

Man has surpassed all He-man, Super-Man
Unfortunately forgot to be a true Human,
Ended up becoming Robot Machines, fearless
Emotionless, Heartless, utterly useless.

Where on earth are leaders and preachers?
Where are Vivekananda kinds—philosophers/thinkers,
I can scarcely find Gandhi's visions and visionary
Real motto, missions and missionaries.
Vasudev Kutambakam is the need of the hour
Global world—a fragrant fresh flower
Its petals—Hindustan, Pakistan, UK, US etc,
Brethren in arms, with love and peace.
United World and united Universe!

Nirmal Rathore Bikaner

PURSUIT OF A FRIEND

Hundreds and millions people we meet in our lifetime
Some are different, some like us, self styled,
All human being are individual personalities
We all are in pursuit of a friend a unique personality.

Life is happening, fun or mundane
Speeding the gears, counting years game,
One and all busy in their own rooms or ways of life
All in a pursuit of a friend, husband or wife.

Human possess bundles of talents and characteristics
Attracted or detested by choice and statistics,
Mr X or Ms X treats themselves perfect
Boast of brains, beauty and pursuit of friend who's perfect.

The friendship, relations seem perfect initially
Few days, months, years, relations strained partially,
Heated arguments, self point of view-invariably
Pursuit of a friend, goes for a six, finally

The friends fare better than husbands and wife
The couple sometimes dragging love, bondage and life,
Sacrifice self-demanding individuality and space
Huge expectations, so, huge problems they face.

The joys and sorrows are two sides of a coin
One should understand, feel sentiments and join,
If can't change spouse, try to adjust and fit
Forgive and forget-friend, end the pursuit.

Hundreds of treaties, deals done in history
Unknown, callous people are united in history,
Diminish your ego, attitude, give life a chance
Anyone, everyone can be your friend
The pursuit ends, smiling in arms.

I, ME, MYSELF IN MORNING BLISS

(Green Lawns Complimented with flora and fauna)

I, me, myself in morning bliss is mesmerizing with serenity
The wonder of nature, unfurled—and its varied activity,
I am lucky to live-life every moment, after moment
Witness the drop of flower, by tender touch of butterfly.

Every morning is dream like, reveries one after the other
Sight of squirrels playing hide and seek, woodpecker or king
    fisher,
The dancing of colourful butterflies and chirping of birds
The romancing roses, poppies, candy tuff or chrysanthemums.

Unlike today's life of hustle bustle and alarming
Supersonic speeds, no time for love and darling,
I feel my heart beats, every nerve and veins throbbing
Sense my senses, solacing the souls and mind crossing.

Silence is bliss, golden opportunity to be with self
Experience calm and tranquility within, be with oneself,
Different world of varied colours and happiness
Rejuvenating like a fresh flower, blooming to glory.

The orange sun beams on dew drops reflect all colours
The soothing chill, and the mild wind bless the dwellers,
The tender green grass feels felt like or velvet
The soft fragrance of petals feels like heaven.

As the sun goes higher and the time flies faster
The reality checks in the beautiful dream like atmosphere,
Birdies, butterflies and the flowers fumes and fragrance
Disappear slowly for another days' appearance.

My little heart starts beating faster than time piece
My reveries fly, also the thrill, transcendence and mental peace,
The hot air balloon ride seems to be over
The dreams deserts, reality bites over and over.

I, me, myself—engrosses in mundane routine
Home, heart, social life's—daily discipline,
Running pillar to post, whole day on toes
Yearning for morning bliss far, from the maddening crowd and woes.

FABULOUS FALLACY'S

The bold and the beautiful, fast and fabulous
Than art man! the stallion, nevertheless,
Half the times in dreams and reveries—Walter mitty
Thou art divine! Herculean and witty.

The young vivacious—visionary
Voracious readers, with big missions and missionary,
From golden age to—today's turbulence
Let all grief be replaced by exuberance.

A secular, philosopher, philanthropist
Some ascetic or agnostic, but some atheist,
Others dedicated, devoted, seldom diabolic
Sacrifices self, leads a role-heroic and symbolic.

Calmness, tolerance and attitude of gratitude
Is thy true nature, learn to live in solitude,
Conviction, character, confidence is your strength
Enthusiasm helps and transforms man's conscience.

The super sensitive man commits fallacies
The foibles, peccadillo and few follies,
The rise of mortal—to a shining star
Or man succumbs; fall—like a withered flower.

The protagonist faces severe tragedy
He's a mere marionette, as if in comedy,
The kingmakers, mighty sultan's and kings
Suffers the hapless man-just like a bird without wings.

Lord! save the soul of samaritan
Forgive him for his blunders, he's smitten,
He's a pure, happy soul on a journey
Forgive him for his fabulous fallacy.

Nirmal Rathore Bikaner

MAKE EVERYDAY SHINE

Make everyday shine, make everyone smile
Live in moments, enjoy—go on extra mile,
Count your life in seconds, minutes and hours
Life is so beautiful and bountiful, forget years.

Make everyday shine, make every one smile
Let your zeal and exuberance—make everyone smile,
Laughter is the best medicine, let's give smile
To the bereaved, heartbroken, poor, old and fragile.

Gods given treasures and pleasures to one and all
Every human is given job, performance, role,
Love, luck, pride, dignity and designation
Create joy and happiness, thrill and jubilation.

Luxuries, comforts unlimited extravaganza
Is like usurping needy one's fortune
God has ushered, blessed you with boons
You be grateful pray for human who are doomed
Make everyday shine, make everyone smile!

GREAT INDIANS ON FRENCH LEAVE

Indians are the most workaholic genre
Reputed politician, bureaucrat, also common gentry,
Famous and prestigious IIT's and IIM's Institutions
Churning out geniuses—brainy and intellectuals.

The leaders, preachers and most of politicians
Lead and speak well, mastery as magicians,
But some great Indians believe and take French leave
Ransack the system, paralyze the power and belief.

The white collar gentleman, the bureaucrat
Practical, logical and efficient, yet some are brats,
Power corrupts and absolute power corrupts absolutely
Great Indian bureaucrats on French leave, occasionally.

The white approned doctors—are true saviors
Sacrifices self and luxuries, avoids class, creed barriers,
Dedicated souls of human beings, clones of God's
Yet some great doctors, protest in strikes and proceed on
    French leave.

The Indian soldiers of defence service class
Full of dignity, valour, patriotism-class apart,
Gives yeomen service, with grit gusto and discipline
Always on duty, never ever think of French leave.

The teachers, counselors, educationists
Grooming the young minds-shaping as perfectionist,
Delivering knowledge and enriched experiences
Yet some teaching commercially at coaching institutions.

The parents—The well wishers, strong pillars
Forget their own ambitions and talents, become healers,
Loose their own identity, for the sake of young ones
Never on leave, not even French ones.

The common gentry—the country men
Does anything possible for his mission, mansion or den,
He's the boss of his mood's, whims and fancy
Great Indian may reach France on his French leave.

ART PIECES & MASTER PIECES

Art pieces and Masterpieces of Gods and deities
Lord Ganesha, Buddha, Krishna and his Gopi's,
Creating ripples by enormous imaginative images
In gold, silver, resin, marble, canvas, paper since stone ages!

Lord Ganesha worshipped foremost in the beginning
Man created hundreds of idols, images and paintings,
With most versatile faces, features and figures
The artifacts of fascinating trunk, mouse, sold in big figures!

Lord Buddha—the prince, ventured in search of peace
Became inspiration for millions, now adorned as masterpiece,
Meditating under bodhi tree, depicting different moods
Eyes so expressive, generating food for thought.

Lord Krishna—the ultimate savior
Gave us Geeta gyan, reason to live and die for,
The flamboyant God with flute, mesmerizing with a smile
Radha and Gopis floating around all along the mile.

Expression and depiction of Krishna is divine
Good looking glowing face and eyes, curly locks,
The charioteer for Arjun's war, his sole warrior
The Thriloki Nath, adorning Sudharshan Chakra

Lords and Gods have extended their positions
From temples, idol places to common men's imaginations,
He wants divine blessing, support ushering everywhere
So the artists have created deities Art Pieces and Masterpieces

MOVIES—
THE MIRROR OF SOCIETY

Movies, films, theatre are the mirror of society
They entertain and educate with cause, lots of variety,
There's exaggeration with extravaganza, unlimited
Yet projects and reflects human psyche, emotion, well edited.

Latest flick—'Force' John Abraham as tough cop
Dedicated police force, yet feel helpless, ministers on top,
Displayed the negative and corrupt gangsters and smugglers
Ransacking the paralyzed system, might and muscle power
　　　of burglars.

Yet another eye opener was movie—Murder 2
Exhibits the bizarre, maniac tendencies and getting away too,
The fully armed and powerful cops, committing suicide
Common young man—a flamboyant taking on the real big fight.

'Arakhshan' was on caste based reservations
Friends turn into foes, shame for today's generations,
'Big' B—the genius, took a Herculean job
Threw open challenge to parasitic coaching tom's.

The youth is thoroughly baffled and disillusioned
Yearns to learn and experiment, but left with illusion,
Dreams of a perfect life, but endanger in strife
Life's battle seems to be won by chicanery not chivalry.

'Gujarish' by Sanjay Leela Bansali—the ace director
Projected euthanasia and grit to face death,
Physically handicapped, though mentally robust
Disabled live and realize life's value; try their best.

Nothing is impossible for daring brave hearts
Sense, sensibility is unique, sharp as a dart,
The indomitable spirit and exemplary will power
Creates ecstasy in catharsis or a catastrophe.

The highly appreciated movie 'Black' was legendary
The challenges and charisma of blinds—is complimentary,
Dark world without colours and beauty of nature
The visionless genre imagines, visions like creator.

The physically, mentally fit people give up easily
Normal human's behave strange and frenzily,
Gods benevolence not enough, crave for more and more
Forget their duty, deity, purity of soul.

'Rang-de-Basanti'—was a patriotic master piece
Youth educated on freedom struggle by modern style for
    harmony and peace,
Rediscovers vigor and enigma of by gone era
The lessons learnt from British Raj, freedom fighters aura.

Movies, films, theatres are truly mirrors of society
Freedom of speech, projection, exhibition—no one's propriety.

Nirmal Rathore Bikaner

SAVIOURS and SURVIVORS

Behold—the saviours and survivors
The fantasies and fury of Gods unfurled,
Don't dare to beleaguer the cosmos and nature
or Gods process of creations and creatures.

Mankind is obsessed and juvenile complexed
Seldom knows his good or evil; is perplexed,
Creates—enjoys, destroys just for fun
Plays with humanity, lives with guns.

The saviours-performing Herculean task
Endangering themselves breathing through mask,
Life is beautiful, bountiful and glorious
Make it heaven on earth—be victorious.

Most of the population—the inhabitants
Leads an honest life, no irritants
But for the few, anti social—militants
Harass the society—country as assailants.

The survivors—only have true knowledge
to live peacefully and happily, talks a pledge,
To make this earth—a beautiful planet
Enjoy to the fullest, sing song or sonnets.

FAST & FABULOUS

(On KARVACHAUTH)

Fasting for Karvachauth, is an old ritual
Hubby like God—whole day being spiritual,
The wives wishes for togetherness for seven incarnations
The husband yearns for seven different persons.

The morning is blissful with madam's synergy
Best of attires, loads of jewellery and energy,
The tinkling of bangles, sparking of Bindi's
The queen-today is regal, generous and fabulous.

The family pampers and cares for her tempers
Celebration time for one and all members,
The preparations for gifts, done well in advance
Best of diamonds, kundans, sarees bought in advance.

The display of ostentatious and extravaganza
The shopaholic's spree, shoppers bonanza,
Special offers for Special Day Queen
Love, luck, pleasantries showered on 40's or teens.

By noon, half the makeup and energy gone
The moon's far away—forlorn,
Hubby's manage their patience and plight
Solaces, swears, just for day, holds her tight.

At four the first pooja of karvachouth performed
All dedicated wife's together pray and thali exchange,
Sings and dances to glory—youth and old
The story of a sister of 7 brothers is told.

Few hours later, the desperation starts
The body seems dehydrated and sinking hearts,
For loving husband—the darling wife
Takes several oaths and swears for amorous life.

Finally the moon God, seem bleakly through clouds
The kids, along with hubbys shout, loud,
All rituals followed—lovingly and religiously
The queen of hearts, takes a sip of water—finally.

Indians believe in celebrating occasionally
Be it Diwali, Christmas, Eid or Holi,
Festivals occurring almost fortnightly
We must cheer and cherish each day—brightly.

WORLD FROM CHILD'S EYES

This World has lost its glory
Let's start a brand new story,
A tender child—with big dreams
Innocent eyes, full of tears, scared of screams.

Sand houses; transformed into huge mansions
Life full of love, roses, no more tensions,
Childhood wishes and dreams cherishing
The kido works and is flourishing.

Adolescent age is the funniest
Full of attitude, ideas most craziest,
He thinks he's too smart, sky is the limit
Relies on everyone, but takes all the credit.

Dignity, valour and high spirits
Endurance and benevolence with no limits,
This world has got its glory
Let's sing a brand new story.

Of a boy whose regained his faith
Love one and all, take a real great oath,
I'll make my India—shining
My world worth living and blooming.

The politicians, ministers during their job
Without any scams, frauds and flops,
The bureaucrat not cutting the edge
Working hard, remembers the pledge.

The forces of our country is supreme
The best of officers, with full discipline,
The grit and the gusto—unmatchable
The spirits and valour—unfathomable.

The Gurus ought to be like Dronacharya
Saintly, well read ; not just Acharya,
Janta Janardhan to behave and live well
Make this world—a Heaven; not hell.

CROSSROADS OF THE JOURNEY

Human being passes through roads and crossroads
Tons of decisions; experiences loads,
Travelling the destiny's route, eternal journey
Varied paths to follow—truth, ambition, money.

Man, oh man! Live gracefully, no regrets
Set a paradigm, live and prosper, don't fret,
Be genuine-not pseudo or pseudonym
Set landmarks and milestones, do the introspection.

Health, Wealth, love, luck is a must—Honey!
Laughter is the best medicine—lets be funny,
High aim aspirations—high expectations
Move on for our real voyage—the expedition.

One road leads to contentment and satisfaction
Other one treads the difficult destination,
The next one challenging and mysterious
The last one enjoyable and adventurous.

The journey is truly rewarding and explorable
The traveler-musketeer's visit memorable,
Mother Earth, nature replete with energy
Complete harmony and cohesiveness—synergy.

The grass on other side is always green
The competitions, rivalries, jealousy felt and seen,
Man and women ogle at each other's fate
Beware! You mortal, before it's too late.

MARRIAGE

(Best Compromise)

Marriages are made in heaven.
The Bride and the groom on seventh heaven,
Or gliding over on cloud nine
Enjoying all rituals on D Day—All is fine.

The story starts from the crucial hunt
Oh no! not with guns, pistols, or stunts,
But with yellow rose for friendship
Progressing into—the perpetual courtship.

The lover and the beloved, drenched in love
Perfect life, perfect size, eyes like dove,
Face like moon and persona shining like sun
All similes, metaphors used for fun.

Story proceeds to the Day of engagement
Princess decked up, perfect arrangements,
Prince Charming, exchanging rings-well fitted
Vows, pledges, promises—unlimited.

Amorous looks, vibrant fleeting moods, beating hearts
Dreams—fantasy—fairy tale marvels,
New visions—new missions, lots of travels
New life, new wife, welcomes and farewells.

Marriage is tying knots of two hearts
Unique bondage with full freedom of thoughts,
The hubby dear—the boss of the house
The gracious lady—queen of the boss,
After few days, months or years
Love vanishing, peace in pieces.
Some couples are lucky, but 100% is seldom
Free and carefree, manipulating freedom,
Marriages are truly made in heaven?
The bride and groom still on seventh heaven?
Or sliding down from cloud nine?
Enjoying or enacting—all is fine!
'God Bless the Brides and Grooms'

HONOURS & TITLES MISPLACED

Our Indian citizens loaded with talents and spirits
Knowledge, values, merits, resources unlimited,
Awards, rewards, incentives rendered on celebrations
Sometimes honours, titles misplaced, faulty felicitation.

Our great politicians, ministers, states persons
Enjoying unwanted, undeserving security by special force
    personals,
As an Indian in this democratic nation
Why treated special, than common man; why this discrimination.

Some of our bureaucrats—bestowed with perks and
    paraphernalia
Using their power, corrupting the system, enjoying regalia,
Files, flowers, bills, committees—all in vain
They manipulate and negotiate all for—self gain.

The defense services—the soldiers is ninety nine percent
    deserving
But for that one percent, the society's ill effect showing,
The Sena Medals, citations, appreciations all true to life
Param Veer Chakra, Kirti and Shaurya Chakra's
    presented posthumous (after life).

The Padma Shree and Padma Bhusans—showering on
    Bollywood stars
And a crore gifted to IPL cricket star,
But for a martyr or a victim, just a few Lakhs announced
Who's lost his life for nation—all comforts denounced.

The gender bias kill the spirits and soul of women
They can approve better than their counterpart—Man,
But for reservations of OBC's and backward classes
All should be equal, justified, whatsoever for general masses.

The tycoons getting richer every day
The poor survives on poverty stricken daily pay,
The NGO's trying their best efforts and luck
Serving humanity with humility, but some sucks.

The democracy of India is ultimate
The discipline, ethos, system of institutions is great,
Our country men are humane—soul mates
But for few who, indulge in coal gate, Rail gate—

Lord—Shower your love, luck equally
Mortals live with high aims, esteems and ideals,
Let there be peace, justice, purity of souls
We live happily—ever after—The ultimate goal.

DISASTER IN DIVINE LAND

Life cycle goes in full circle, starting from birth
Living, growing, performing all rites—till death,
New incarnations, new identity, a new name
Its as simple as changing attire, with new aims.

Divine blessings showering on every mortal
Difficult situations and disasters, though turned fatal,
The blessings or curse is weighed depending on our doing
The karmic cycle decides one's fate or destiny.

The sacred shrines of Kedarnath and Badrinath are divine
The pilgrims, tourists, visit the terrain—rough and unkind,
The voyage becomes last homage—turns devastating and
    volatile   .
Gods message to mankind; pray dear—once in a while.

The strong belief, devotion, makes the journey possible
In spite of hazardous journey; missions impossible,
The old and fragile, the tiny tots and their delicate mother
Crossing all odds and obstacles, challenging the weather.

God balance the ecological system, pressure on earth
Kalyug plays hide and seek, ruining and destroying,
The cloud burst, deluge is symbolic of Gods fury
Mankind ought to decipher the cues and clues of God's Jury.

Disaster in divine land is indeed unfortunate
Lets Learn to live with love, peace, humility, get blessings and be
    fortunate,
Save mother Earth, its inhabitants and environment
Lets take an oath to save and restore nature, supporting the
planned projects of government.

MET A NEW FRIEND—JUST MY CLONE

Met a new friend-off late; just my clone
I see my mirror image-heart, spirits, zeal of my own,
My heart may be larger, but her beauty and looks
Bold and beautiful, fast fabulous and gorgeous.

The first shining smile gave signals of friendship
The style, poise and panache-suited my companionship,
Confident and attitude with a perfect balance
Centre of attraction, though with carefree elegance.

She's full of life—a true enthusiast
Passionate and perfectionist, blooms with fun and zest,
Good heart and soul, along with beauty and brains
I got a friend, what I imagined and dreamt myself;
    a perfect dame.

Loving partner, perfect hostess—a true connoisseur
Working to the limit, though a diehard party lover,
Lives life on own terms-indoors or outdoors
Smiles giggles, laughs to the fullest, enjoys dance floors.

I met a new friend off late, just my clone
Loves self, hubby, family, home, even pets and dogs,
Life becomes beautiful and bountiful in her company
God bless this new friend, sweet as symphony.

TWENTY YEARS OF TOGETHERNESS

(20ᵗʰ Anniversary)

In one's life, marriage is necessary
Having an adorable life partner is compulsory,
We are, on top of the world, a great chemistry
Twenty years of togetherness, our 20ᵗʰ Anniversary.

First five years were roller coaster ride
Best of best combinations, sailing with the tide,
Newly weds, the perfect memorable time
The unforgettable, lovable, all is fine.

Next five years, blessed with cute babies
No time for hubby, self, just changing nappies,
Love takes a back seat, lots of responsibility
Girl to wife, to mother is truly great responsibility.

Love transformed from self to hubby, now kids
Yesterdays kid-we, yelling our kids wake up sid,
Trying all tricks, rules, formulas
Sorting out kids life, bribing pizzas and colas.

Next five years, is ambitions and togetherness
All working, in different directions and faithfulness,
Now child is the father, daughter soothers
Everyone realizes the importance of money matters.

Twenty years of togetherness 20th anniversary
Couldn't believe, life is speed and its machinery,
Looks like dream, a fairy tale
Yesterday we met, today 20 yrs a lovely tale.
Life's fun, magic, full of miracles
Wonderful fantasies, dreams and fables,
Live with love, faith and dignity
You are the creator of your destiny.
Long life to our bonding and togetherness
We love and are loved to madness,
May lord bless us on this day
May every day be special like Anniversary Day.

IDENTITY & ORIGIN

Being Indian, Hindu, names, surnames matter
Does American, African, Britons really differ,
Human—anatomically are same still, I wonder
Do we have some identity and origin, I ponder.

Continents, countries, caste and creed; vary
Religion, rituals, traditions and values do vary,
Personalities, characteristics, nature will differ
Faces and features, fortunes may differ.

God's creation is amazing, every mortal unique
Different countenance, ideas and identity and aims,
Different origin, opinions, values and whines
But actually God sons—Heart and soul are some.

The Indian, Britons, American, African are all humans
Their colour may differ, but the colour of blood is same,
Vital organs, senses, same—sensibility may differ
Gist of religion is same—spirituality may differ.

Principles, doctrines, philosophies, governance may differ
But gospel of truth, honestly, integrity will not differ,
Fate, destiny of every mortal is different
But God's justice for every human is well deserving.

To take pride in identity and origin is fine
Being human, son of God—all brethren,
Identity—gives you chance to prove to be unique
Origin—gives you better chance of your past, present and future.

Realize and recognize your great birth and identity
Let other take pride in your personality and originality,
Live for others and let others live peacefully
That's your true identity and personality and originality.

MY PARENTS—PILLAR OF MY LIFE

My parents, the quintessential of my life
Next to God, fully devoted, strongest pillar of my life,
I am blessed to be chosen as their daughter
I am indeed the luckiest, life full of laughter.

My father is a legend, icon-a personality
Magnanimous visionary, full of dignity,
Voracious reader, a man of golden words
Chivalrous leader owns lot of swords.

Zeal and valour is his true being
Best father, true husband, ideal human being,
Love with warmth and emotions is his true nature.
He's bigger than life with real great stature.

Mom—my dearest is like Kohinoor
Most precious, purest, worth many crore,
Compassion, devotion, sacrifice in abundance
Charismatic, confident, full of elegance.

Unconditional love, unlimited forgiveness like a Queen
She's an ultimate 'Ma' divine like a dream,
She's not only my Idol, a woman of substance
But my whole world, universe and cosmos.

My parents—my life line, full of benevolence
Perfect 'Pa, Ma', personalities—par excellence,
Ushers affection, blessing, nectar of life on me
God's magnificent marvel and gift for me.

May God bless them with joys and happiness
Reward them for their extravagant greatness,
May their life be full of flowers and blooms
Shine their luck with hundred Suns and Moons.

My wish, yearning, a passionate prayer
Miracles, charisma happens through prayers,
Lord bless all Moms and Dads and their loved ones
With loads of love, luck, success and fun.

HANDSOME HUNK

My handsome-hunk, my hubby darling
As a holy man with a halo, always smiling,
Makes my day and my life-worth living
He's the reason for the exuberance and happy living.

Best hubby, father and a perfect human being
His wishes, visions, dreams, no less than a king,
He's royal, loyal, with abundant morality
Can't challenge and compare his conviction and simplicity.

Striving for perfection, aiming for success
Positive attitude, dexterity and prowess,
Contended to the core, zealous—a complete man
Camaraderie, chivalry, no less than Super Man.

Ideal aims, rightful pathways leading triumph
He a spirited soul—the triumphant,
A dedicated soldier, Samaritan—the saviour
My true friend, guide and philosopher.

A philanthropist, virtuous and angelic
Yet full of love, so very romantic,
As they say handsome is that handsome does
Lives life king size—yet with a cause.

He's sweeter than sugar, smarter than Tom cruise
Adventurous than James bond on his cruise,
He's loving than a lover, caring than mother
He's my prince charming, my true soul soother.

Lord shower your blessings on us
We live with love, dignity and luck
Happily ever after.

Nirmal Rathore Bikaner

'MOM THE DEAR'—EPITOME OF LOVE

'Mom' the dear is the epitome of love
Affection, compassion, unconditional love,
Caring, nurturing, unlimited forgiveness
Pampering, blessing and cheerfulness.

Untiring efforts from day one
Smiling, giggling, mimicking just for fun,
Doing all big and small jobs
Changing roles, attires or tops.

Living in a dream or utopian world
Magic and mysteries unfurled,
Unexpected situations and conditions
Sometimes funny or deadly positions.

Yearning for aspirations and hopes
Hoping against hopes, holding life's ropes,
Deserving more than ever
Running from pillar to post even in fever.

When the going gets tough-
The tough gets going,
The ocean of life may be rough
The self may go, but the child is the crux.

JOY—MY LIFE LINE

(Bundle of Joy)

Joy—a bundle of happiness
My strength, my spirits and luckiness,
The tower of pride and tolerance
The power of love abundance.

Innocence filled in his beautiful big eyes
The smile, the dimple bounds the ties,
The countenance, vigour of his face
Gives me immense speed and pace.

Honesty, integrity is the crux line
Being naughty and funny is still fine,
Joy-my package of luck, my life line
Benevolence—par excellence in today's time.

I look forward for a future Maharana Pratap
Luv, Kush or Lord Shri Rama,
The great warrior Karan or Arjuna
or the ultimate saviour—Lord Shri Krishna.

MOM'S BLESSINGS

(bundle of happiness)

Dhananjay—my second son
Blooming with love, caring and loads of fun,
Adolescent, mighty strength and naughty smile
His shooting height with souring great profile.

Happy (go lucky) is his pet name
He yearns to be a Richie Rich and is fond of fame,
Wants to discover, and develop new empires
I wish him good luck! for his dreams and desires.

Wings of freedom and flights of fantasy
He's full of life, not the least fussy,
Utopian ideas he can materialize as real
Only if you serve him good cuisine and great meal.

Intelligent, sharp, like Elephants memory
But loosing temper is only moms worry,
Great player, stable body with stable mind
Truly deserves all accolades and praises
I wish him to be a winner—A triumphant.

NECKLACE—THE MARVELLOUS'

(Gift from hubby-The beginning of my Poetic expression)

The glowing piece of art and jewel
With diamonds, kundan—so real,
Its Cut clarity, Colour and carats
With solitaires, princess or long begets.

The queen of Sheeba imagined and dreamt,
I too, like Queen Victoria felt,
The amazing, dazzling danglers,
The beautiful glittering pendent.

The glowing piece of art and jewel
With diamonds, kundans—so real,
Brought glow on my rosy cheeks
Made a crowning glory in just a week.

My handsome hubby darling
My loving prince charming,
Gifted this kundan necklace
A masterpiece—so marvelous.

My love, blessings and gratitude,
Full with awe, less the attitude,
My life with him, shines like a star
I flourish and bloom just like a flower.

God Bless.

DUKE & DUCHESS

(Would be names of my pets)

"The more I understand human beings
The more I love animals",
From childhood; growing up to adolescent
I always possessed pets, dogs, now—Duke and Duchess.

After marriage, life was amazing, differently dealt
No time, space, need for pet/dog was felt,
Then the blessings of God ushered as kids
Again no time, space, need for pet/dog was felt.

Today at forty five, husband, kids all settled
Lots of time, space and utmost need for pet is felt,
Hubby busy with his career, kids seldom need pat
All I am left home alone, yearning to love and pat.

Though I am busy too, like a honey bee
The queen of the house, delegating jobs, holding keys,
A versatile person—people generally call me
Busy in my world of—poetry, painting and all possible 'ings'.

Some days starts with walking, shooting, Golfing
Other leisure days—shopping or gallivanting,
In my boredom, loneliness, I wish to talk and express my feelings
I feel my Duck and Duchess can fill the vacuum and be thrilling.

Every morning will be playful and joyful with new routine
Every morning long walks and jogs on the green,
The lovey-dovey darling the new pet—member
Understand all emotions and expressions, love they remember.

The duke and duchess yet to be our family member
I am desperately waiting for the new born's eyes to open sooner,
Planning for their needs and comforts, like a new born baby
Nervous and excited to share their responsibility.

The more I understand human beings
The more I love animals!

46ᵗʰ MILESTONE 26ᵗʰ JULY 2012

Life starts at forty, its rocking on 46ᵗʰ milestone
Independent, free lancer, boss of my own,
Though sweet heart of one and mother of two
Life's colourful as vibgyor, no fuss, no blue.

Life in the army, they say is pretty fine
Nowadays in NSG, Manesar is simply divine,
First class citizen of India, living in Delhi
I am like Queen Elizabeth, enjoying extravaganza.

A fantabulous life partner with all paraphernalia
Great visions, missions, new horizons and galleria,
Pride and valour, Adventure and thrill-unlimited
Anything on earth is possible, with commando's camaraderie
    unlimited!

Dignified job as lecturer at Amity college
Delivering lectures, displaying talent and knowledge,
The shining eyes and the sparkle of youth
Kindle my spirits and vigor to ecstasy, oh you.

From dawn to dusk—life is fulfilling as a dream
Action, reaction, challenges, performing as a team,
New ventures, new ambitions—no dead lines
Volunteering, competing with self—no bindings.

Workaholic along with shopaholic is the mood
Aim for perfection, no worry or hurry for food,
Work hard and eventually party harder
Is my motto of life, oh ya partner.

Life is pleasure, treasure to cherish
Success, ambition, hope's—all flourish,
True love triumph—all dreams come true
Life is truly—rocking at 46ᵗʰ milestone.

YOU ARE YOUR OWN SOUL MATE

In the happiest moments of our life
In the midst of tranquility or laughter of our life,
You are your own soul mate—man
Even in tumultuous time, one gets solace by self—Yo man.

In meditation, prayers or hymns
One is in communion with God & himself,
In the midst of grief, sorrow or despair
You are your own soul mate, only you have to bear.

The karmic cycle goes on and on
Be rich or poor, young and old, moves on,
But for the benefit or brunt of one's planetary placement
You are your soul mate facing God's judgment.

The friend philosopher, guide is our intellect
Heart & soul plays vital preacher—in fact,
Mind riding on seven horses, reins in all different directions
Man—you are your own soul mate, in spite of loads of affection.

HUMAN RELATIONS

Human beings are like social animals
Likes to develop, new friends, new relations,
Through ages, as mortals history
Without companion life's a boring territory

With a friend, we enjoy live better & longer
Share, laugh, cry, learn, imitate & behave somber,
No restrictions on emotions & passions
No sorry's and thank you's—Be yourself! Great lesson.

As a spouse we learn to compromise & sacrifice
Love to the limits, pledges on sunsets & sunrise,
Feel the loneliness, importance of togetherness
Feel the warmth of love, caring & bondedness.

As parents, it's an ultimate experience
New life—so tender soft & our own impression,
Life revolves around this bundle of Joy
From adulthood to old age, he's the real toy.

SOULMATES

Life—the most pious & purest blessing of God!
Love-life's most wonderful passion blessed by Lord,
The heart and soul clicking & beating in harmony
The soul mates with passionate love & amorous looks,
    result in ceremony.

Every breath reminds us of life force energy
Lovers passion, reason for life, create synergy,
Lives on pledges, sacrificing self for soul mate
In mesmerizing, meandering meadows, date after date.

Lovers lane is a labyrinth, like the locks of hair
Oblivion of the world, living in their own paradise they dare,
For the love sake forgets and forgive one & all
Become recluse or rebellion, depending on the call.

The lovey-dovey couple completely drenched in each
    other's eyes
Sparkling smile and twinkling shine as fire flies,
The tender touch of breeze on the flowing locks
Adorned by a beautiful rose, bud or flocks.

ROBOTIC LIFE CYCLE

Life is a boon and blessing of God
In nature's arms blessed by Lords,
Fascinating flora and fauna with blooming dales
Divine hands, replete with ecstatic arena, or aisles.

Human beings-the greatest creation of God
Lives, loves, enjoys in their childhood phase,
Laugh and cry without any rhyme or reason
Innocent mischief's, smiling now & then, no treason.

Adolescents believes in extremes
Either on cloud I, or flat on mother earth,
Either over workaholic; or over lethargic lying beside the hearth
Fully love striker, or totally; no love lost.

Mortals—as mature man & women are unique
Lives, loves, laughs-as routine; so robotic,
Some hot headed with cold shoulders & thick skinned
Some cool as cucumber, yet so routine-cut, copy, paste as it
    filmed.

The monotony of lovers, regular phrases
Same type, templates, set for messages,
The adjectives, similes, and metaphors
Cry for change of feelings and flowers.

The parents love & affection is purest as gold
Duty into death, unconditionally they care greatness unfold,
But for their progeny, sometimes fail
Over obsessed by self career ; or robotic trail.

The robotic life cycle takes a turn
Child becomes father, mother, sacrifice he learns,
Careless & callous is replaced by dedication
He does anything & everything, with full devotion.

Life is a boon & blessing of God
In Nature's arms, blessed by Lords.

ALICE IN WONDERLAND

In the midst of Delhi's maddening hustle & bustle
Stands an Oasis, Manekshaw Centre, a castle,
With it sprawling green lanes and landscaping
I felt like Alice in wonderland, architects design & planning.

Named after a great general Manekshaw
Gave us victory in great Bangladesh War,
The Asoka sthamb, a great matter of India's Pride
The interiors, flower arrangements as if for a special bride.

The journey starts with a romantic ambiance
The natural beauty with birds, peacocks & butterflies,
Amidst the trees, flowers, hover's-a man made wonder Helicopter
    seen
Just landing to pick me up for another world; 7th heaven.

As we approach gate luxury & extravaganza unlimited
Beautifully painted roofs, embroidered panels & chandeliers
    lighted,
Massive statues of Gods, marvelous art & artifacts
In silver, bronze, brass, stone, marble-super architects.

Suddenly reached the foyer, crossing the fishes diving in water
Mysterious, meandering ways, leads to other quarter,
Painted gates of caves like design, one wonders
I really enjoyed like Alice, with new, new wonders.

Every nook & corner takes us through ages of history
From Ramayan to Mahabharat days, unfolding mystery,
The concept based peacock décor was amazing
Peacock in colour scheme, theme-design was worth witnessing.

Like Alice, I too adventured in wonderland
With my prince charming, the front & rear of this peaceful hamlet,
I wish I could live here & enjoy forever
The lavish lawns—as if Eden garden & be happy ever after.

FREEDOM & LIBERTY

Luxury, and extravaganza amuse us
High post, salary, perks allure us,
Freedom is, essentially our birth right
Liberty is foremost, as heart, soul & breath.

As in nature, the free flowing breeze & waterfalls
Touches every heart, living on earth, be it summer or spring fall,
The sight of sun, moon is amazing, so are clouds & stars
For a person caged & claustrophobic behind bars.

The values of liberty is realized after its gone
For a child, under strict laws, liberty torn,
For a lady newlywed, bound by duty & rituals
For a man, who's jailed, because of wrong allegations.

Ask the true meaning of freedom, from a victim of hijack
Ask the spirit of freedom from child, who lacks,
Know the meaning of freedom from patient with ailments
Know the true spirit of freedom from nation-not independent.

Freedom of speech, belief and religion
Liberty of thoughts, values or profession,
A sovereign nation with free will
An independent country, progressing all have their wish & will.

Liberty is as vital as heart, soul & breath
Freedom is essentially our birth right.

THE AWESOME COUPLE-SO SIMPLE

Simplicity is the greatest trait
Of personality and character, till date,
Being human, humane & humble is difficult
My parents possess all these—I sincerely felt.

A successful leader, commander, had a happy team
Every officer, individual got freedom, high esteem,
Being gentle as the boss-at the helm of affairs is difficult
My parents possess all these-I really felt.

A pleasant nature and an encouraging smile
Live & let live, happily & peacefully, no tensions pile,
Being a friend, philosopher & guide is difficult
My parents possess all these—I honestly felt.

Tall, dark handsome is a Mills & Boon hero
Man with command, conviction, confidence is real hero,
Being untouched by ego, attitude is difficult
My father, possess all these, I sincerely felt.

Bold & beautiful, fast and fabulous are catchy words
Golden heart full with compassion & affection more than words,
Being simple, yet smart & sophisticated is difficult
My mother posses all these, all these, I really felt.

My parents-the most humble couple, I've met
They are so inspiring, encouraging, appreciating you bet!
We all can learn & unlearn few important lessons
Adopt simplicity like them-the greatest & the most difficult lesson.

God bless this awesome couple!

ZODIAC-MY LUCKY CHARM

Zodiac-my Lucky Charm!
He's my darling—so adorable & smart,
My walking, talking, listening, fun partner
He's my two year pet white & cinnamon coloured Labrador.

Zodiac-my Lucky Charm!
Arrived on eleven, eleven, eleven,
The most auspicious day in recent years
He's a bundle of joy & thrill, love & care.

Zodiac-my Lucky Charm!
With his expressive eyes, nodding left, right his head,
Waging his tail, jumping to & from fully exited
He's a misguided missile-full throttle, if not controlled or checked.

Zodiac-my Lucky Charm!
Gives me love, company when I really need it,
He's is first listener of my poetry couplet's
Sits so close, feeling the warmth, sleeps in seconds, close
    eyelids.

Zodiac-my Lucky Charm!
His arrival was welcome, well timed,
He's the baby of the house, fully pampered not spoilt
From dawn to dusk, he's the toy of the house.

Zodiac-my Lucky Charm!
His feelings, understanding, expressions are amazing,
He's a real stress buster, so entertaining
He' my true, best friend—indeed!

FACE BOOK

Human-young or old, rich or middle class
Male female, all are hooked on face book alas!
Just as the eyelids open, mind still sleeping
Modern technocrats, searching on face book,
    before bed tea sipping.

At morning bliss, they sit on computers
Before breakfast, or jogging few kilometers,
Crazy excited idlers-wasting hours on face book
The craziest are the Youth—avoiding syllabus & text book.

The ordinary lad or lady wants to be celebrity
Clicks, up loads, photos, text, likes etc; misusing facility,
They are oblivion of living standard or status, but update
    face-book status
The desperation linger on and on for internet access.

The ambition, profile, aspirations are sabotaged
The real values, precious time, kept as hostage,
The burning issues, concerns of country ignored
This generation smiles, giggles for camera—and is floored.

God save this earth from people with narcissus complex
Self praise, selfish motives & gains, still perplexed,
I, me, myself is the latest formula
I am . . . . I did . . . blah-blah-blah.